Praise for *You Don't Have to Die to Go to Heaven*

"Susan Allison presents an ancient roadmap to the heavens in a way that we can all employ to visit the realms beyond death. In this journey, we discover that there is only life after life and that we can map our destiny consciously in this lifetime and the next!"

—Alberto Villoldo, PhD, author of
Shaman, Healer, Sage, and *One Spirit Medicine*
and *A Shaman's Miraculous Tools for Healing*

"An increasing body of evidence suggests that the survival of consciousness following bodily death is real and that it is possible to have a preview of what lies ahead. In *You Don't Have to Die to Go to Heaven* Susan Allison shows how."

—Larry Dossey, MD, author of *One Mind:
How Our Individual Mind Is Part of a
Greater Consciousness and Why It Matters*

"Dr. Susan Allison's book is a blessing and breakthrough for humanity. The book helps to overcome the fear of death and to understand the circle of life by visiting heaven with the help of guides from the spirit world. With compassion, inspiration, encouragement, and heartfelt teachings, every sentence of this book is extraordinary insightful, transforming, and supportive."

—Eva-Maria Mora, founder of Quantum
Angel Healing and Cosmic Recording

You Don't Have to Die to Go to Heaven

You Don't Have to Die to Go to Heaven

....

*How to Find Guidance and Healing
in the Spirit Realms*

SUSAN ALLISON, PhD

WEISER BOOKS

This edition first published in 2015 by
Weiser Books, an imprint of
Red Wheel/Weiser, LLC
With offices at:
65 Parker Street, Suite 7
Newburyport, MA 01950
www.redwheelweiser.com

ISBN: 978-1-57863-588-7

Library of Congress Cataloging-in-Publication Data
Allison, Susan (Therapist)
  You don't have to die to go to heaven : how to find guidance and
healing in the spirit realms / Susan Allison, PhD.
       pages cm
  Includes bibliographical references.
  1. Shamanism. 2. Trance--Religious aspects--Shamanism.
  3. Spiritual life--Shamanism. I. Title.
  BF1621.A56 2015
  201'.44--dc23
                                        2015035775

Cover design by Jim Warner
Cover photograph © Twomeows/Getty
Interior by Howie Severson
Typeset in Goudy Old Style

Printed in the United States of America
MG
10 9 8 7 6 5 4 3 2 1

Contents

*This book is dedicated to my husband Thomas
Hansen Hickenbottom (1947–2013), who
inspired me during nineteen years together,
and who inspires me now. It is also dedicated
to my children, grandchildren, ancestors, and
all the loving spirit beings that have supported
me to write this book. Thank you all.*

Introduction

I will love spring again, but not today. Only seven months
since you closed your eyes and never woke, since I left our bed
for a sip of coffee, a bite of muffin, and when crawling in
against your warm body, found chest still, breath gone. So
it's too soon to feel joy in all this beauty and fruition. Alone
in Eden, I ask, how can the world be this bright, without you?

—From my poem "How Can the World Be This Bright?"

If you have ever loved someone deeply who has passed
away, you understand how I felt on August 3, 2013
when my husband stopped breathing. Even though
he had been sick for six years, I don't think anyone is
ever ready for that moment. I know I wasn't. It is hard
enough going through the emotional pain that on some
days feels like a freight train in my chest, but there is
also the realization that he is not coming back, that life
will never be the same, and that this life is stretching
slowly into forever.

Without my family, friends, hospice, and my shamanic journeywork, I do not think I would still be
alive, and even if alive, I wouldn't be sane. Now, two
years after his death, I am beginning to see more light

and feel more hope in my life, and writing this book has been part of my recovery. I am so grateful I can go into trance and do shamanic journeying to receive help from my spirit allies, and I can even spend time with my husband in a level of heaven. What a gift to know that the energy between us is alive, that our infinite spirits can commune in a heavenly world. What a gift to know without a doubt that he is immortal and happy, that I am immortal, and so are you.

Not only can I journey to meet my husband and other loved ones in spirit realms, but I can visit angels, helpers, ancestors, guides, and teachers in shamanic worlds. One reason I've written *You Don't Have to Die to Go to Heaven* is to help you learn to journey to spirit realms to connect with your own loving allies. In the chapters that follow, you will learn how to do shamanic journeying step-by-step, and in the process, realize you are immortal, as are your departed loved ones. You don't have to die or have a near-death experience. You can spirit travel to other dimensions right now, and receive insights to guide and heal you. As a dividend, you will realize you are not alone, but always have caring spirit beings to love and support you.

Unlike ancient times, when only the shaman of a tribe journeyed to spirit worlds, you can now learn to do shamanic journeying on your own. Traditionally, the shaman went into an altered state by listening to a drum or a rattle, and spirit traveled to other worlds to retrieve information for the tribe or an individual. Then the shaman returned from the trance with messages and tools from the spirits to help tribal members. In essence, the shaman was and is the spiritual leader of a tribe. Shamanism is the forerunner of all religions, with an ancient spiritual tradition and practice dating back about 60,000 years. Although tribal life has changed over thousands of years, shamanic practices still exist in Siberia, Lapland, Africa, Australia, Peru, Chile, Mexico, Alaska, Hawaii, and other places.

Now you have the opportunity to listen to a drumming recording and journey to other dimensions. There you can meet with spirit allies and loved ones for insight, guidance, and perhaps for physical, emotional, or spiritual healing. You can not only receive support during journeying, but you can also overcome any fear, especially the fear of death. I know from the direct experience of doing shamanic work since 1993, going on thousands of journeys, and visiting departed friends and family, that spirit worlds exist, including a level of heaven. If you have any fear of your own transition, worry about your departed loved ones, or perhaps doubt that an afterlife exists, read on!

While doing trance journeywork, I have met my grandmother, whom I never met in this life, and can visit my parents any time. I have met with human and animal allies, guides, and teachers such as Lao Tzu, Jesus, Mary Magdalene, Rama, Ganesh, Arianrhod, St. Francis, a Pawnee Chief, Eagle, Swan, and four angels. Because I have personally visited three spirit worlds and connected with so many loving beings, I am looking forward to my afterlife.

Since my husband's transition in 2013, I have journeyed to a heavenly realm where we walk on a beach, dance in the moonlight, swim, and explore the levels of heaven. After being with Tom during my journeys, I return feeling reassured and happy. Yes, his physical body is gone, but our spirits are immortal and can be together any time I choose to visit or feel his energy. It would be an honor to help you connect with your departed loved ones, and in the process, help you discover that death is not to be feared, and it is not the end.

You may have several reasons for reading this book: perhaps you are mainly curious or no longer want to fear death; perhaps you want to connect with power animals, spirit allies, guides, and teachers; or perhaps you want to learn how to visit loved ones in spirit realms. You may also want to look at your life in new ways, to shed what no longer works and embrace alternative ways of seeing yourself and relating to others, new ways of living your life more fully and joyfully. You can achieve all this by reading the text and doing the exercises, including the shamanic journey.

Shamanic journeying involves listening to a repetitive sound, such as a drum or rattle, and going into a relaxing trance that allows you to disassociate from your physical reality and spirit travel to other dimensions. Listening to a drum or rattle is a bit like a meditation mantra that helps you go into an altered state and have visions. Most commonly, I use recorded drumming to journey, and you can download drumming music from my website at *www.drsusanallison.com*. The monotonous beating of the drum can take you into a brain wave called "theta" that researchers say helps achieve a higher state of consciousness and can facilitate a visionary experience.[1]

While in a shamanic trance, you will not be visioning through your conscious mind, but through the subconscious, utilizing all your senses and emotions. Thus, a journey is undertaken with the subconscious leading, and the trance unfolds effortlessly when you engage all your senses to capture the experience. You aren't seeing and exploring through the rational mind, but through the heart. All wisdom from spirit beings comes in first through the heart and is then processed by the mind to help you decipher and integrate what occurs on the journey.

If you have ever meditated, done yoga, or practiced other ways of relaxing the brain and nervous system, such as deep breathing, being in nature, or listening to music, then shamanic journeywork will feel familiar. Anything you have done to calm your mind or feel more peaceful can assist you to journey. The specifics of how to go into trance and the details about each spirit world will be covered in the following chapters.

The spirit realms are actually parallel universes that also have been called "the other worlds" and "the dreamtime." These places are not in our heads, not in our imaginations; they are alternate dimensions of reality. Indigenous peoples and shamanic teachers agree that these worlds are organized into a Middle World, a Lower World, and an Upper World with more than one level in each realm. In the chapters that follow, you will be able to journey to these worlds.

The Middle World is the focus of chapter 1 because it is important as a central place to journey to the other realms, like a launching pad to the Upper World and a subway station to the Lower World. The Middle World is the most like ordinary reality, and is like a dream aspect of this world. In this text it will be called the Middle World, your personal place of power, the sacred garden, or your natural world. It may be a place in nature that you have seen, or it may be somewhere new.

I've found that the Middle World is a refuge, a place where I feel at peace, and when meeting with loving spirits, it is where I am encouraged. This place of power is yours and everything about it supports who you are and what you need. When you journey to the Middle World, you'll find that everything can communicate with you, and the messages will come into your mind.

The Lower World of chapter 2 is often described as pure nature, and in my experience feels ancient and primeval. Those journeying describe caves, deep valleys, cliffs, mountains, seas, rivers, jungles, forests, and deserts. To me, this world is raw, pristine nature that has not been affected by humans. The Lower World should never be confused with hell, even though some people think that "going down" means the underworld of the Greeks or the hell of Christians. It is neither. It is Nature itself. The Lower World is especially important because you will meet animal helpers that can facilitate travel to the Upper World and a level of heaven.

The Upper Worlds, as presented in chapters 3–7, may seem similar to descriptions of Mt. Olympus or heaven, and there are similarities. The Upper Worlds are more ethereal and luminous than the other worlds, and are reached by passing through clouds, mist, the sun, or another substance. Here you may find avatars, gurus, guides, teachers, ancestors, angelic beings, palaces, temples, and crystal cities. You can also meet your soul family or divine teachers, or experience a past life and connect with departed loved ones. It is here that I meet with my parents and my husband as well as Jesus, Mary Magdalene, and Socrates. Going to the Upper World always uplifts me, and I smile knowing that we can go any time, and that we don't have to die first!

I call one Upper World "a level of heaven" because of the lofty beings that appear. This higher realm is, I believe, just one part of heaven, and the one we can visit while still embodied. During a shamanic journey, I saw other levels of heaven above the one I can visit. I now agree with passages in religious texts that describe levels, and even cities, in heaven. Not until seeing these realms above me did I fully believe in their existence. This is what is incredible about journeywork, because you have a direct experience of these dimensions and needn't rely on others to describe them. You discover them for yourself.

Like a treasure hunt, you can begin your discovery by reading the following chapters in order, building your confidence and your journeying skills as you spirit travel from one world to the next. The format in each chapter is experiential, with a personal check-in, a real life practice, shamanic journeys, questions to help you process your journeys, and a final exercise that helps you turn insight into action.

I feel an energy rising from this page to the ones that follow. It is a pathway, a trail of golden coins that you pick up as you go until your pockets are full, until you are filling a treasure chest and even the chest is overflowing. You are an explorer on a sacred quest to discover your own inner holy grail, a cup that never fully empties. My own treasure is the knowledge that I am serving you, and am fulfilling my own soul's purpose. My greatest wish is that as you read, you release any fear about your own transition or about where your departed loved ones have gone. As you journey, may you find all the guidance and healing you need. It is my honor to travel with you.

Personal Place of Power

My feet know the way, feel
each grain of sand and tree root,
each leaf of fern on the trail.

Warm wind brushes my face
lifts my hair; red and yellow parrots
call to each other in the canopy
of green light, welcoming me.

I am alone, yet not alone.
Everything is alive and
calling me home.

—From my poem "Calling Me Home"

The poem that opens this chapter describes one of my recent places of power in the shamanic Middle World. However, my first journey to find my sacred garden was far different:

> As the drumming begins, I walk a winding path in dense jungle for what seems like miles. It's the middle of a moonless night and everything is in darkness. Still, I keep going and eventually wend my way to a tiny, dark, perfectly arranged Zen garden. After the length of my journey, this simple garden is a welcome sight. However, it is so precise, gravel raked in careful patterns and plants pruned in sharp angles, that I feel hemmed in and stifled by the perfection. It is still dark and I can't find anywhere to sit. So I just stand there self-consciously and try not to disturb the gravel designs. A high rock wall surrounds the garden and this makes the space seem even more claustrophobic. I feel trapped.

I felt disappointed by my first journey to the Middle World. It didn't feel like a sacred garden where I could feel at peace and find renewal. Later, I realized why this had been my experience. This perfect Zen garden was symbolic of my current situation. At the time I was teaching and feeling I had to do it perfectly. Also, I was tired of this profession and felt depressed, hence the small space, high wall, and darkness. My life felt constrained and rigid. Now I understood why I had a tiny Zen garden. This was my life.

After this journey, I made plans to leave teaching and expand my therapy practice. As soon as I set this change in motion, I felt more expansive. I refused to be such a perfectionist and stopped driving myself crazy by setting such impossible standards. Soon after making these changes, I did another shamanic journey to the Middle World, secretly hoping I would find a different place.

I find myself in a different setting, not a jungle, and it is daytime, not night. The light is dim at first, but I ask for more light and it gets brighter. I am walking in a forest of hardwood trees, and in front of me is an arched bridge that spans a stream, like the ones in Japanese gardens. Ahead is a white gate covered in vines and flowers, and beyond the entrance is a large garden with wild nature around it, with a beautiful sprawling tree. To the right and down some steps are a river and a bench, and off to the left, a pool and a waterfall surrounded by tropical trees and ferns. I feel ecstatic as I explore this amazing world.

What I realized after this experience is that when I change my real life in the outer world, my inner shamanic world also changes. Your personal place of power is symbolic of your real life, and when you alter your life, your garden changes; when you change your garden, your ordinary life transforms. To illustrate, as I created a more ideal professional life, my shamanic world felt more expansive, with more room, variety, more color and light. This new sacred place also felt more welcoming, with a bench to sit on and a tree that invited climbing. I would also meet loving spirit allies to help me in my everyday life.

Purpose of a Place of Power

One purpose of having a personal place of power is to provide a refuge for the spirit to go immediately after death. At the time of death, the person is less confused and frightened, knowing there is a familiar sacred place to go. In my therapy practice I have helped terminally ill clients journey to their personal places of power to feel more at peace about their deaths. Dying does not seem as daunting when you know you will be arriving in a familiar world and welcomed by beings that love you.

A seriously ill client shared his journey to his place of power:

> I'm at a white gate to an amazing garden that looks like my grandmother's, but even more lush. As I enter, I see my mom and dad and two favorite uncles, and they are so happy to see me. The garden is filled with lilacs and roses, and has a gazebo and a hammock. I lie down in the hammock and let the warm wind rock me.

Tears fell as he described the beauty of his garden and the relief he felt when seeing his family. For many months he journeyed to his place of solace, and according to his wife, died peacefully without fear.

Having a sacred space is not only helpful at the time of transition, but can give you respite and support while still alive. Once you've found your place of power, it becomes a sanctuary where you feel at ease.

Like meditation, journeying to a spirit realm offers the brain and nervous system a break from the hectic pace of our world. You can return from these visions feeling renewed. A former client said this after her first Middle World journey: "I feel so relaxed, grounded, and full of purpose."

Also, visiting your natural world can give you new ways to change what no longer serves you. You can return feeling more conscious, more evolved, and able to live from your higher self instead of the ego. As an added blessing, you can ask for and receive healings in your garden and return feeling lighter and healthier.

The main reason I feel better after journeying to my place of power is that beings that love me are there to offer wisdom and support. These allies have been elements, such as water, trees, and clouds, as well as animals that can communicate with me. Mostly, human spirit helpers come to my place of power and graciously guide me.

Your own experiences will be unique to you, and your journeys will be different from mine, but they will be exactly what you need. Whether you hope to dispel your fear of death, relax from daily stress, receive guidance from spirit allies, or feel more empowered, transformed, or healed, journeying to your sacred place will enrich your life. In this chapter you will be guided to discover your place of power, and you will invite in caring spirit beings. In the process you will realize that you are not alone, and that you are loved more than you know.

Check-In

At each step of the way, with each meditation or journey, you'll have an opportunity to check in with yourself. Choose a journal to set aside for this purpose. It's a good idea to mark the book page number and a keyword or two in your journal to remind you of which exercise you're writing about. I also find it useful to date my responses to meditations or journeys. The following is your first check-in.

Why do you want to find your own place of power?

What are your feelings about death? Would you like a familiar place to go to after you die?

How do you feel about meeting beings that love you in your sacred place? Is there anyone you hope to meet who is now in spirit?

How stressed are you in your current life? Could you use a time-out in a peaceful place while journeying?

Does anything need to change in your life?

What in your body, mind, or spirit may need healing?

Before You Journey

As mentioned in the Introduction, you can go to my website, *www.drsusanallison.com*, and download drumming music to use while you journey. It would be helpful to do this now before reading further.

Intention and Protection

For this journey to the Middle World, the intention is to find your path and travel to your personal place of power. This is a realm that could resemble a garden or any natural setting. You may discover that you've been here before, or the location could be new. Don't try to think of a place beforehand. In fact, as you take deep breaths, let go of your rational mind that wants to control and plan. Just trust that your subconscious mind, heart, and intuition are creating the experience.

Also, you can ask for protection as you travel. This doesn't mean that journeying is unsafe, but it's a way to ask for assistance and feel supported as you journey. Whatever your spiritual beliefs, you can call on anything to guide and protect you. Some people hold a special stone that feels grounding, or light a candle. A simple request might be: "Please help me journey to my personal place of power and return safely."

The Way In

Sit or lie down comfortably, and make sure you won't be disturbed; if you tend to fall asleep easily, you might want to sit up. Next, put on an eye mask or scarf to block the light, and begin to relax. Take several deep breaths, breathing in positive energy and breathing out anything limiting.

Begin listening to the drumming recording, and with eyes closed, set the intention to go to your place of power in the Middle World. First, imagine yourself on a path, knowing whatever path shows up is the right one. Letting go of your thoughts, use all your senses, such as sight, hearing, feeling, and sense of smell to experience where you are. Take in this beautiful place. In this relaxed trance you are magical and can ask for the perfect temperature, time of day, and amount of light you want. Walk slowly and take in everything around you.

If at any time on your path or in your place of power you feel as if you are controlling what is happening with your mind, just stop and retrace your steps back to where you were before the mind took over. You want to allow everything to unfold naturally, with your senses fully engaged and your subconscious guiding you.

Let yourself arrive in your place of power effortlessly, again using your senses to see, hear, smell, and feel what is around you. Once in your natural world, look around and explore your realm. Take in everything in order to write about it later. Remember you are magical and creative, and if you want water, it will appear. If you want a comfortable place to sit, it will instantly manifest. Notice what time of day it is, the quality of light, what season it seems to be, how warm or cool it feels, and whatever else you see.

You might want to settle somewhere that looks inviting. Sometimes it feels good to close your eyes and allow yourself to be nurtured by this magical place. If you need guidance or healing, you can ask this natural world for what you need. Perhaps a tree feels especially supportive, or a body of water, or the sky. Let yourself be filled up. Everything in the Middle World can communicate with you, so don't be surprised if you hear a message in your mind.

While listening to the drumming, there will be a fast beating "call back" to let you know it is time to return. Thank your sacred place and express that you will be back. Breathe in all you see and sense and begin walking your path back to where you began.

When the drumming ends, take a few deep breaths, and feel yourself coming up out of this Middle World and back into ordinary reality. Move your body, stretch, and feel yourself coming all the way back. Open your eyes. It's important not to come back too quickly, and it also helps to drink a glass of water afterward. Feel the liquid flow all the way down, grounding you as you plant your feet on the floor.

· ·

Check-In

Answer the following prompts in your journal.

Describe your path.

How might your path be symbolic of your life path in some way?

Describe your sacred place in nature.

Did you magically change anything?

How might your personal place of power be symbolic of your life?

Did you receive any guidance or healing?

If you received any messages, write about them.

•••

Symbols and Metaphors

Now re-read what you wrote down with the intention of seeing any further metaphors or symbols that may be important in your real life. Pay close attention to such things as the time of day, the season, how much light there is, the size of the space, the type of terrain, the kinds of trees or plants, if there is water, if you saw animals or humans, even shadows or shapes, and anything that seems of value. *Everything* is important and has a message for you!

Recently, in a shamanic circle, a woman shared her journey and its symbolism:

> *I find myself busting through walls of cobblestones, like an ancient defense around a city, but I burst through them easily and scatter these rocks away from me. I walk freely through the hole and find myself in a field where a caveman sits waiting for me. He tells me I need to learn how to do everything myself, not to*

depend on others any longer, and teaches me how to start a fire with flint until a blaze is roaring. He says the time has come for me to embrace my power and to be fully in my own life, dependent on myself.

She also commented that although she's still a wife and mother of nearly grown children, it's time to focus on her own life and come into her power.

Think back to your recent journey. Do you see any additional symbols or metaphors about your life?

Loving Spirit Beings

I cross a wooden bridge and open the gate to my garden where fragrant flowers are blooming. Ferns are bright green and light streams from golden sun. I climb down to a lower level and sit by a stream and waterfall.

Looking up, I see the waterfall part and a woman steps through. She is veiled, yet my sense is that she is my father's mother. I never met my grandmother, Sara, who died before I was born, but she walks over and sits with me. She throws off her veil and her long auburn hair falls in curls down her back. I notice her beautiful long fingers and white hands as she reaches for mine. I feel an immediate connection, realizing how alike we are, and how grateful I am to finally meet her.

My grandmother was with me for several years, and one day when I traveled to my sacred place, she was gone. She had served her purpose as my spirit ally, and I had learned all I could from her. What she gave me is the confidence to be myself and to follow my heart. You, too, have loving spirit allies just waiting for you to invite them to join you. This is the purpose of the next journey.

In preparation, you can think about anyone now in spirit you would like to see, knowing they may or may not appear. I had no idea that my grandmother was one of my spirit allies, and I feel blessed that she chose to come. At times I ask people to appear, and at other times I just let the magic unfold and surprise me. Just follow your intuition about whether to request someone or not.

In general, spirit allies can be with you for a short time or for years, and often move on once their purpose has been served. You may meet departed family members or friends, departed pets, ancestors, descendants, beings you have never met that are assigned to you, spirit animals, nature spirits, and even the elements of earth, air, fire, and water. The perfect spirit allies will come.

When they do appear, here are some possible questions to ask:

Who are you? What is your name?

Why have you come?

Do you have any wisdom for me?

Check-In

Who are your loved ones, including humans and animals no longer embodied, that you would like to see? Remember that they may or may not appear during this journey.

Intention and Protection

The intention for this journey is to travel to your place of power and invite in a loving spirit ally. For protection you can say something like, "Please help me to journey to and from my place of power safely. Thank you."

Spirit Ally Journey

Follow the directions above to get ready to spirit travel to your place of power, including starting the drumming recording. With eyes closed, listen to the drum and imagine yourself on your path to your natural world. You now remember how your path and garden look and feel, but if you have changed anything in your real life, your sacred place may also be different.

Once in your place of power, invite in beings that love you. At times your spirit allies will come in human form, and sometimes they appear as holograms or pure light. Occasionally, you won't see them at all; you will just hear their voices. One or more persons or animals may appear, or the elements of nature may be your allies. Remember that everything can communicate with you in your mind.

Spend time enjoying your helper's company, asking any questions or just listening to shared wisdom. I like to ask their names, and why they have come, and I try to take in everything about their physical appearance to research later.

When you hear the drumming speed up, say good-bye and thank your spirit ally and find your way to your path and back to your starting point. Take a few deep breaths, stretch, and, when ready, open your eyes.

• •

Check-In

What does your place of power look like this time?

Who or what appears when you call? What happens between you?

What are the questions you ask, or what messages do you receive?

Is there any action you can take in your ordinary life based on this wisdom?

Do you notice any metaphors or symbols about your life from the path, your place of power, or from your encounter?

• •

Research

If a loving spirit ally has shown up in your natural world, you can do research on this individual, animal, or elemental. This being may be someone in your family, like my grandmother, that you want to know more about. On the other hand, you may not recognize this individual, but if you remember his or her name and appearance, you can research them.

My first spirit beings in my place of power were my grandmother and a winged snake. I did research on both, and the results were fascinating, especially in terms of why these beings were in my life. I found that my grandmother was an artist and a visionary and also wrote poetry and stories. She has helped me have the confidence to paint, write songs, and feel comfortable with my psychic abilities. My winged snake was my guardian and companion, and similar to the cobra over Buddha's head, protected me.

Other spirit helpers have appeared to me in the tropical world described in the above poem. Two of my allies are a Pawnee Chief and St. Francis. The Pawnee Chief has a Mohawk haircut, and I once argued with him about being Pawnee. Then when I did research, I found that Pawnee Chiefs wear their hair in that manner. I apologized to him and felt very humbled. This is the main reason to do research, to support what you experience with your allies.

Now is a good time to write any research findings about your spirit allies in your journal.

Teachers in Your Place of Power

I see my grandmother sitting on the bench next to the river. Next to her is a man with shoulder-length grey hair, brown skin, and when he turns to the side, I see he is Asian. The two of them are talking in hushed tones and laughing occasionally. I say hello, and he very humbly greets me with a nodded head, but no words. Looking more closely, I notice he is wearing a robe of green and blue silk. I have no idea who he is so I ask, "Who are you and why are you in my garden?" He says softly and sweetly, "My name is Lao Tzu, and I am your gardener."

Our spiritual teachers instruct us and help us make changes in our lives. Often we do not recognize our helpers, and this was certainly true of my first teacher, Lao Tzu. I realized fairly quickly that he didn't mean he would be pruning my bushes, but pruning me! He came to help me trim the parts of myself that no longer worked. He came to help me become more humble and grow.

In doing research, I find that Lao Tzu (meaning Old Sage) was keeper of the archives in Chinese court, and that he left when he was around eighty years old, disillusioned with humanity. Before departing, he left his inspiring text, the *Tao Te Ching*.[2] I apologized to Lao Tzu for being rude during our first meeting. I wish I had spent more time with him, for he is no longer in my garden.

If any being appears and gives you a name, as Lao Tzu did, be sure to look up the person and write down anything that seems relevant. Even if you didn't ask for them to come, they are appearing to serve you, and some shamanic teachers say they have been assigned to you. The other lesson is to appreciate them each moment, because teachers do not always stay with you forever.

Intention and Protection

Your intention for this journey is to travel to your Middle World and invite in a teacher. For protection you can say what works for you or something like this, "Please help me travel safely to and from my garden where I will invite in a teacher. Thank you."

Inviting a Teacher

Prepare as you have in previous journeys and start the drumming recording. As you listen to the drum, imagine yourself on your sacred path to the Middle World. Remember your intention to meet a teacher, and find your way to your personal place of power.

Once there, explore a bit and see if anything has changed. When it feels right, invite in a teacher to join you, and expect someone to come. Once this spirit being arrives, begin a dialogue, either asking questions or asking your teacher to share insights with you. Enjoy this time together and remember everything that is shared.

When the drum speeds up, say good-bye, thank your teacher, and make your way back to your path and where you began.

Taking several deep breaths, bring yourself back to ordinary reality, stretch, and, when ready, open your eyes.

Check-In

How does your sacred place seem this time? Has anything changed?

If a teacher arrives, describe this being.

What is your teacher's name and what did you learn about this person, either from their appearance or what was shared?

What questions did you ask, or what wisdom did you receive?

Is there anything you wish to change about yourself or your life?

•••

Research

If you do any research on your teacher, record your findings in your journal.

Guides in the Garden

I see a tall, stunningly beautiful woman wearing a long silver gown with a silver pendant around her neck. She has long dark hair that curls past her shoulders to the middle of her back. She holds out her hands to me and smiles the most radiant smile as she tells me her name is Arianrhod. I hear her speak in my head, "All you

envision is already unfolding, and will come to frui-
tion. When you need me just say 'shining silver wheel
of radiance, come to me, come to me.'"

Guides such as Arianrhod are different from spirit allies or teachers, because these wise beings have been with us through all our incarnations. In general, allies are helpers and protectors, and are often comforting and loving and feel like good friends. Spirit teachers train us, often about how we can change our defects into assets. They can help us be teachable and shed what no longer serves us. Guides often seem more formal, more enlightened, timeless, and all-knowing, and they immediately begin teaching us lessons that are important for our soul's growth. Arianrhod, Jesus, and Rama are my sacred guides, who say they have been with me forever.

Arianrhod has been with me since 1994. In my research I found that Arianrhod is the goddess of personal destiny and a Welsh moon goddess worshipped by the Celts.[3] She tells me to watch the moon in all its phases, and I can bask in her light and feel her working through me as a muse.

Jesus is an avatar and healer, who teaches me about compassion and love, and who has taught me how to heal myself and others:

I am in pain, my shoulder practically knocked out of
its socket by a cycling injury. I decide to journey for
help and arrive in my natural world. There, near the
tree, is a huge stone table, like ones used as altars or
for sacrifices. I know I need to lie on this flat stone. I

look up into the face of Jesus, who tells me that He will
do a healing on my shoulder by bringing in golden light
from God. He will do so if I promise to help anyone
who comes to me in pain. Jesus says to receive and
know that He is with me always and will help me be
of service.

Rama is a god in Hinduism who appeared quite
unexpectedly, and who continues to teach me to stand
in my power and fulfill my purpose:

I meet a man named Rama, who tells me he has been
with me in all my lifetimes. He is a turbaned, dark-
skinned Indian with gorgeous, soulful eyes who takes
my hands. I feel love and light fill my heart. He calls
me "pupil" and says he is trying to help me become the
best I can be in this life. I tell him I want to change,
and he says all I need to do is set an intention with
passion, and it will come true.

In my research I find that Rama is the incarnation
of the Hindu god Vishnu. Rama has been worshipped
since the eleventh century for being a model of right
action, reason, and all the virtues.[4] He is definitely a
teacher I need in my life, and is the main guide assigned
to me for all my lifetimes.

Check-In

In thinking about your own life, its issues and challenges, what might a guide help you with at this time?

···

Intention and Protection

Now it's time to meet your own guide and receive guidance from this wise being. Try to leave your mind open to the mystery and magic of this process, and allow the universe to provide the perfect guide for you and your life.

Also, ask for protection, that you be held in safety as you journey, and that you return enriched and transformed in some way.

Journey to Meet a Guide

Start the drumming recording and, with eyes closed, set your intention to meet a guide. Imagine yourself on your path and walking easily to your natural world. When you arrive, invite in a being to guide and teach you, and then meet with this person. Notice his or her attire, ask the individual's name, and perhaps ask why this guide has come into your life. If you have something specific you need help with, ask about it, or just listen for shared wisdom.

When the drum speeds up, thank your guide for coming. Find your way back to your path and the place where you began the journey. Take several deep breaths, stretch, and breathe your way back into your body and into the room. When you are ready, open your eyes.

••

Check-In

Does your place of personal power look the same, or has it changed?

Who or what came as your guide? Describe this being.

What happened between you, and what messages did you receive?

How can you use these messages in your real life?

••

Research

As you have done previously, do research on anything you are curious about from your journey and write your findings in your journal.

Inviting an Ancestor

I walk to the waterfall in my garden and see an ebony-skinned woman who is very tall and regal, wearing a headdress of woven straw in the shape of a crown. She has a bone in her nose and is wearing bone or ivory jewelry around her neck. She looks African, and tells me that she is Tongan, my ancestor, and the

daughter of a chief. She tells me about her life, espe-
cially about being forced to marry, and not being with
the man she loves. Menana tells me that I will become
stronger spiritually and will become a powerful healer,
as she was. We embrace and call each other sisters.

After this journey I did research and found some amazing things. When she said she was Tongan, I thought she meant the island of Tonga, but I found that Tongan people live in South Africa. Also, her name is Menana, which means "drop or walk into" in Hindi. That confused me, but I then found that over 400,000 people from India live in South Africa, and that they came to the country hundreds of years ago.[5] My ancestor could be of African *and* Indian descent.

Also, her name could be symbolic, as she dropped or walked into my Middle World as an ancestor soul. I love shamanic work because the experiences are always supported by actual research. Finding out more about our ancestors, and even our own lineage, is so rewarding.

• •

Check-In

What do you know of your ancestry? What are you curious about?

How do you feel about "surprises," finding a new ancestor and culture?

• •

Intention and Protection

The intention for this journey is to travel to your place of power and invite an ancestor to join you. For protection, you can say what works for you.

Journey to Meet an Ancestor

Relax and ready yourself for journeying. As the drumming begins, imagine yourself on the path to your place in nature. Using all your senses, find yourself arriving in your natural world and explore. Now invite in an ancestor and have a conversation. Enjoy your time together until the drumming calls you back. Say good-bye and thank your ancestor. Make your way to your path and walk to the starting point. Take a few deep breaths and, when ready, open your eyes.

• •

Check-In

Has anything changed in your place of power?

If an ancestor appeared, who is this person? Describe your ancestor, including their name, attire, and culture if possible.

What did you share?

Record any research about your ancestor.

• •

Journeys from Your Place of Power

Not only can you journey *to* this natural world, but you can embark on journeys *from* here to other realms. The Middle World is like an airport so you can travel to all the other spirit worlds. Briefly you will be shown how to journey down to the Lower World and how to travel to the Upper Worlds. Specific journeys to these other realms will be taken in the chapters that follow.

> *In my place of power I dive into a deep pool and am able to breathe easily underwater. As I surface, I am in an underground cavern with a door in the rock wall. I walk into a room where women dress me in white buckskin and put feathers in my hair and a turquoise necklace around my neck. Thirteen grandmothers sit in a circle around a fire and I know I've been here before. They give me a bouquet of wildflowers and tell me to sit in my place in the south. I am told to throw everything I want to shed into the fire and I do so using pieces of wood. I feel cleansed as I release the past.*

If you have a river, lake, ocean, or pool in your sacred place, you can dive in and swim to another level in the Middle World or to the Lower World. I find I can breathe magically under water just like a fish, and so can you. If no water exists in your place of power, you can ask for some and it will magically appear.

You can take trips from your Middle World to other levels in that realm, and will do so in the chapters that follow. You will also learn how to find other ways to journey to the Lower and Upper Worlds from your place of power.

Ways to the Lower World

Think about your place in the Middle World, especially noting if there are trees, mountains, caves, and water. The usual way of traveling down to the Lower World is through a hole in a tree, a cave, a pool of water, a hole or opening in the earth, and any place where you descend. If you don't have such a portal, you can magically create something just by thinking it. Then in chapter 2 you will be ready to travel from your place of power down to the Lower World of animal helpers.

Ways to the Upper World

Your sacred place in the Middle World can also be how you travel to the Upper Worlds. Do you have a tree, plateau, or mountaintop in your place of power? If none exist, you can magically intend them into being. Having a "Great Tree" in my place of power has helped me reach the Upper Worlds for many years. I recommend asking for such a tree if you don't have one now. Chapters that follow will describe the Upper Worlds, and you can choose to start in your own garden.

Insight *to* Action

What could you do to create a more fulfilling life, based on the realizations in this chapter?

The Beginning

Rather than this being the end of chapter 1, it is actually the beginning of your adventures to realms beyond the Middle World. Having your personal place of power creates a safe haven, whether for relaxing or for meeting spirit allies, guides, and teachers. It is also the gateway to all the spirit worlds, including heaven. I wish you *bon voyage!*

~ 2 ~

World of Animal Helpers

I need to soar alone tonight
into black sky
find a solitary peak
build a nest and sleep;
feel fierce wind buffet every side
and when lonely look up at silver stars
at three-quarter moon illumined pink;
know I'm not alone
am held by rock
by all that breathes.

I listen to raven's call
to mouse's voice
hear lizard teach me oldest truths:
I am air, desert sand
kin to dragonfly and ant.
Midnight stillness tells me
I am one with all that is.

—From my poem "Vision Quest Truth"

I wrote the above poem while on a vision quest in the California desert. There on a high plateau, sheltered by a Joshua tree, I communed with nature, closed my eyes, and journeyed to the Lower World of totem animals. One memory that came to me then was of my first shamanic journey to the Lower World:

I find myself in a railway tunnel walking along rusty tracks for what seems like miles until finally I see an opening. Relieved to be stepping into sunlight, I take a breath and turn to see a camel.

The camel smells and keeps hissing through his teeth. I'm afraid to ask if he is my power animal, and sense I am to get on. As soon as we begin to walk, I start to complain, "Oh my God, this is my power animal?" Just then an enormous bald eagle swoops me up with its talons. I scream in fear and continue to complain until the eagle soars over a swollen river and drops me into its current.

Sputtering and half drowned, I crawl onto a granite rock and lie there gasping. On a stone above me the eagle watches. I hear him speak in my mind, "Are you teachable? Are you humble enough to learn anything? Are you ready yet?" Still catching my breath, I nod my head, and get on the eagle's back. We fly over a red rock canyon with jagged cliffs and valleys. At first I am silent from shock, but again ask, "Are you my power animal? Where are we going? What are you going to teach me?" The eagle reaches the top of the cliff and drops me like a stone into his nest. As he flies away, I *hear these words in my head, "Stay here until you are humble enough to proceed."*

I feel completely abandoned and sorry for myself. I begin to cry and then to feel ashamed of my rudeness. I want to apologize. I feel humbled and hope the eagle will forgive me. As if he could hear my thoughts, the eagle appears and asks if I am ready to begin my work with him. I nod and softly thank him.

This describes my first journey to the Lower World, and what a learning experience it was. Not only did I find the Lower World and my power animal, but I embarked on a training that took years. What I've come to realize is that the Lower World is a place to refine our characters, to eliminate traits and behaviors that do not serve us, and that may in fact be keeping us from becoming the highest we can be. Imagine having hundreds of journeys to all the spirit worlds, and how much transformation can occur. This, I feel, is a purpose of shamanic journeywork: the conscious evolution of our souls.

Check-In

Do you want to refine or eliminate any of your traits or behaviors?

What traits would you like to develop? What kind of person would you like to become?

The Lower World

From my experience, the Lower World is earthy, natural, and can even seem ancient and primeval in its landscape. Also, the main beings that have appeared to me have been wild animals, birds, reptiles, and insects. Individuals in my journey groups have seen mythical animals in the Lower World, like dragons and unicorns, and also have had human allies show up. Occasionally, I have been led by an animal helper to teachers, often an indigenous grandmother and grandfather in a cave. Except for one recent journey to a new Lower World, the setting of my animal realm has remained the same, the red rock canyon described above. What has changed, however, are the ways I get there and the animal helpers that come.

One issue that arises for some people when journeying to the Lower World is the worry that descending means going to a place like hell. If you have any associations with hell when thinking of journeying to the Lower World, rest assured that this is not a place of torment, but a place that is Nature in all its raw beauty. The practice of shamanism, including the shaman's ability to travel to spirit worlds, pre-dates the establishment of organized religion by thousands of years. Shamans worldwide have journeyed to the Lower World for centuries to work with power animals in order to honor them and try to embody some of their qualities. When journeying to the Lower World, you are visiting an ancient and sacred realm with totem animals just waiting to be your helpers.

Your realm of animal helpers will appear perfectly for you. By letting go of your mind and its tendency to predict and orchestrate, you can welcome whatever occurs.

• •

Check-In

How comfortable do you feel "descending" to this Lower World?

• •

The Way In

My first journey to the Lower World began with a descent down a hole in an old apple tree that was partly hollow. I would envision being in the pasture below the tree, then climbing down into the tree and a cave below it.

What works for some people to descend to the Lower World is to choose a tree, a hole in the ground, a cave, or some way into the earth that they have actually seen. Recently in a journey group, one person tried to enter a cave he had seen at the beach, but finally went through a manhole he remembered on a street in San Francisco!

Also, as described in chapter 1, you can enter the animal realm by first going to your personal place of power. There you can use a portal such as a tree, cave, pool, waterfall, or any way to descend to the Lower World.

The Huichol people of Mexico have another way into the spirit world. Once in a trance, you imagine yourself in a field and come upon a fence that you climb.

There, a stag is waiting to carry you to the Lower or Upper World. You might try this way into the spirit world that the Huichol have used for centuries.

Inside the Earth

After entering the Lower World, let yourself travel into the earth. Don't be surprised if you slide on a water slide, fly, are carried, walk down steps, are propelled by a mud-slide, and so on. You are magical, and even if you jump or fly down, you will be safe.

Once inside the earth, which usually resembles a cave, it may take a while to find the exit. Also, the exit could be above you, below you, or to the side; if it is above, you might see light and a trap door or hole. Just climb up and out and you will find yourself outside. Most people find the lighted exit on the same level. Follow your own intuition about which direction to take.

Sometimes you may drop through the floor to another level, swim through water, or find a cavern and a path from there. Just trust that whatever is happening is important and is a metaphor for your life. Someone in a recent group found himself as a mole, digging his way out of the cave. Later he saw that he was the mole trying to dig himself out of a situation. Part of the gift of journeywork is the mystery. Just let it unfold.

Finding the Light

After traveling underground, you will find the light and emerge. It might be a place you have seen before, or it might be somewhere new. Usually, you will find the same Lower World on each journey, but at times a new location and a new experience may await you.

Introduction to Animal Helpers

As I emerge from the cave into blinding sunlight, I ask for one of my power animals to come. The rock canyon is quiet, except for the river in the distance, rushing over boulders. I decide to dive into a pool, and once on shore I dress and keep walking barefoot along the riverbank. Immersed in nature, I don't see the shape to my right until it is right next to me, a fully grown white jaguar that casually walks beside me, flicking his tail and gazing at me with tawny eyes.

The Lower World is the realm of spirit animals, and although some people have seen humans here, the majority of individuals see only animals. Over the years I've been blessed with several power animals, and each of them has a certain gift. Eagle is still the main animal teacher who shows up in my place of power, and he often takes me to the Upper World and to one level of heaven. I have a new animal helper, Swan, who also carries me to the Upper World.

I highly recommend buying the book *Animal Speak* by Ted Andrews. Each time you meet with a power animal or see an animal in real life, you can look up the mythology surrounding it. Andrews has done extensive research into the history and symbolism of each being. *Animal Speak* is my shamanic bible.

As mentioned previously, everything in the shamanic world is magical, including you. In other words, you can create and change anything in your world, and you can also change form, fly, breathe under water, talk to trees and clouds, and hear or sense their messages in your mind.

Check-In

Do you already have an animal, bird, reptile, insect, or mythical being that is special to you? This being may or may not show up as your animal helper, but the perfect one will appear for you.

Intention and Protection

In traveling to the Lower World, your intention is to move through a portal you choose, make your way through the space in the earth to an exit where you see light, then leave the cave and walk out into the world that appears to you. Once in the Lower World, invite a power animal to arrive.

If you want, you can ask for protection or hold a stone that will ground you and help you stay centered during your journey. A request might be, "Please help me journey safely to and from the Lower World where I meet my animal helper. Thank you."

You can also ask that a spirit ally come with you to the Lower World, and if it is dark, you can always ask for more light.

A Lower World Journey

Begin the drumming recording and go into trance as you have done previously. If your mind begins to wander, just bring yourself back to where you were before your conscious mind interrupted, and start again from there.

Follow the instructions above for entering your portal, walking through the earth, and coming out into the light. Invite a power animal to come, see if he or she arrives, and ask, "Are you my animal helper?" After finding your power animal, you can spend time together exploring the Lower World, talking, and listening to shared wisdom. Don't be discouraged if an animal does not appear this time. Just explore this realm and ask for a power animal next time.

As the drum speeds up in a "call back," thank any beings that have shown up, and come back the same way. Usually you can return more quickly than you went, and at times can fly or take shortcuts. Once you are back, take several deep breaths, stretch, and open your eyes.

· ·

Check-In

What was your portal or way into the lower world?

How did you get from the portal to the space underground?

Describe your time inside the earth before you exited.

What does your Lower World look like? Have you been here in real life, or is it somewhere new?

Did you meet a power animal? Describe your animal helper.

Describe the time you spent with your power animal and any wisdom you received.

Was there anything symbolic of your real life on this journey?

You also may want to pick up your journal and record the entire journey in as much detail as possible, using the above questions as a guide.

••

Travel with Animal Helpers

I walk barefoot in sand surrounded by sandstone cliffs. Looking to my right, I see a shallow cave, and inside is a sleek, muscular, satin-coated leopard with green eyes. I lie next to her, look into her eyes, and say, "I want to be powerful like you." She tells me to get on her back and we ride like the wind through stone passages to a large cavern. On a throne is a woman with a jaguar head and woman's body. She tells me she is Jaguar Woman, and says, "You have grown soft and weak like a pregnant rabbit. You have forgotten who you are, have forgotten your power. You need to ride on Stellar to feel her power and remember your own." I climb on the leopard's back and we lope through tunnels and out into the open canyon. Her message to me is, "Remember to own your physical, mental, and spiritual power."

One of the reasons an animal helper comes into our lives is to remind us of who we are, to help us fulfill our potential and purpose. Spending time traveling in the Lower World with your helper will teach you about your strengths, your weaknesses, what you need to develop, and what you need to release that limits who you are becoming. In your journey to meet your power animal, hopefully you have begun a relationship to help you transform and shine.

Intention and Protection

The intention of this next journey is to meet an animal helper and travel with them in the Lower World, as I did with Eagle and Leopard. The animal that is right for you will come carry you on an adventure, perhaps on its back or nearby, as you walk, run, fly, or swim. Be open to the teachings and wisdom of this animal helper as you travel with him or her. Your request for protection is whatever has worked for you previously.

Travel Journey

Prepare for this journey as you know best, start the drumming recording, and be clear in your intention to travel with or on an animal helper. Find your way into the portal, and underground to the exit and the light.

Once you have emerged, begin looking for or inviting an animal helper to appear. When the bird, insect, reptile, or other animal arrives, travel with him or her through the Lower World, in whatever way feels best. Don't forget you are in a magical spirit realm and you are magical here. It is completely possible to ride on a creature that is smaller than you are. It will seem totally natural to ride on the back of a butterfly, hawk, lizard, or muskrat!

Allow time to talk with your totem animal, asking questions and mostly listening to the wisdom they share. Just enjoy your time traveling with your power animal, until the drum calls you back. Say good-bye and thank you, and walk your path back to the beginning and to ordinary reality. Once you are back, be sure to take deep breaths, stretch, and, when ready, open your eyes.

• •

Check-In

How was your trip to the Lower World? Did anything new occur?

If you traveled with your animal helper, describe your experience.

What questions did you ask your animal helper, or what wisdom did you receive?

Was there anything on your journey that was symbolic of your ordinary life? Is there anything you wish to change about yourself or your life?

• •

Shape-Shifting into an Animal

As I enter the Lower World, I instantly become a male snowy owl, lifting into the air and soaring over canyons. I catch a rat, swallow it, and then fly to my nest, where I regurgitate the food for two baby owlets. I snuggle warmly with my mate and babies until just before dawn, and then I fly to the edge of the forest. I shape-shift into human form and climb onto a stag's back. I feel his coarse fur and wide antlers, and wrap my arms around his neck as we run. We reach the cliff's edge, and then we become bald eagles flying into the valley. The two of us rest in a tree and talk about being mated for life until it is time to return to human form. As a woman, I run in a dry riverbed faster and faster, until I feel my legs becoming furry and feel the swish, swish of my long tail. I am a white wolf with a rabbit in my mouth running to a cave. A Native elder sits by a roaring fire. I offer the rabbit and he makes a stew. Soon I hear my wolf mate calling, and I run up the hill- side where the full moon is rising beyond the trees. We sniff noses, tumble into a playful romp, and lie next to one another, our hearts beating fast and strong.

This journey was unusual because I shape-shifted into more than one being: first a male snowy owl, then a bald eagle, and last, a white wolf. From the snowy owl, I learned to be selfless and provide for my family. Also, from all three, I learned what it is to mate for life, to be devoted and loyal to my mated partner. The white wolf taught me to offer gifts to my teachers and to play and enjoy time with my mate.

I have shape-shifted most often into birds, and I have flown many times with my greatest power animal and teacher, Eagle. Recently Eagle reminded me that aside from the animals described above, I have also been a dolphin, a whale, a fish, a mermaid, a jaguar, a cougar, a firefly, a butterfly, and a starfish. From the starfish, I learned that we have the same light inside us from the star nation, the same atoms and energy, but just appear in a different form. Shape-shifting can anchor deep realizations for our greatest growth.

In your previous journeys to the Lower World, you may have traveled on a bird or an animal such as a deer, large cat, bear, and so on, or you may have shape-shifted into a bird, insect, or animal. If not, you can do so in this next journey. There are no limitations in the shamanic world; you can ride on a giant condor or jaguar, and almost better yet, you can become a predatory bird or wild animal.

The purpose of changing into animals is to immerse yourself in their world, to heighten your senses, to feel your body and mind, to sharpen your instincts, to experience worlds you never have before. It is to grow and expand more fully in your human life. Every encounter with an animal helper will give you insights you need. Whether flying as a hawk or running as a cheetah, you can feel the freedom, courage, and power to live your ordinary life more fully.

Intention and Protection

The intention for this journey is to travel to a lower realm and shape-shift into an animal. For protection, use whatever works for you.

Shape-Shifting Journey

Become ready to journey, start the drumming recording, and find yourself traveling underground in whatever way occurs. Find the light or exit and emerge into the Lower World. Once there, hold the intention of shape-shifting into an animal. You might first meet with your animal helper and then shift, or it could occur spontaneously. Just let go of expectation, and let the magic happen.

Use all your senses to feel what it is like to be this animal: your seeing, hearing, touch, and smell; use every sense to actually become this spirit being. Be especially aware of your abilities and remember everything you can to record later. If you get messages from the world around you or perhaps from being this animal, remember these insights.

When the drumming speeds up, it is time to come back. Express gratitude for your experience and to this world and its creatures. Return the way you came, and when fully back in ordinary reality, take deep breaths, stretch, and open your eyes.

• •

Check-In

What happened on the way to the Lower World this time?

Once in the Lower World, were you able to shape-shift? Describe the animal you became and all you experienced.

What messages did you receive on this shape-shifting journey?

Were there any symbols or metaphors in this journey that represent your real life?

•••

Nature Spirits

I walk in the red rock canyon and sense I am to climb up to a cave in the cliff. When I arrive only my grandfather is there; he has me lie by the soothing fire and does a healing on me. Then he carries me up the mountain, nearly floating magically as we rise higher to a snow-capped peak. Grandfather leaves me to commune with the spirit of the mountain, which is the mountain itself. I sit on a seat carved out of stone and let the masculine energy of the mountain fill me with minerals and vitality, balancing my feminine with stronger male energy. I hear the spirit of the mountain tell me to spend more time in solitude, to sit on a mountain or large rock and breathe in its power.

∾

I meet my grandmother in my garden and together we corkscrew down through the earth like a drill, nearly down to its core. We are birthed out of Gaia's vagina, then protected in a large bubble of water in order to travel safely through fire and each earth layer. Gaia's heart is pumping so hard and at times faltering, and we sense that her heart needs love and light, so grandmother and I give her a luminous healing. Afterward her heart seems to pump more steadily and vigorously. We also fill the center of the earth with light and then ascend.

The Lower World is the domain of the elements and all nature spirits. You can journey to the spirit of a mountain (earth) or to the spirit of a river or ocean (water), the spirit of the foundation of the earth where I found Gaia (fire). You can also journey to the spirit of the air or to the spirits of plants or trees. It is your choice—just follow your intuition.

Intention and Protection

The intention for this journey is to go to the Lower World and travel to the spirit of a part of nature, such as earth, water, air, or fire. This might include a mountain journey, a journey to a body of water, a journey inside the earth down to its foundation, or a journey to plants or trees and so on, in order to commune with the spirit of this part of the natural world. For protection, say whatever works best for you.

Nature Spirit Journey

Get ready as you have previously, start the drumming recording, and think of your intention. Find yourself either in your Middle World where you find a way to descend, or envision your portal into the earth. Go down into the cave or tunnel, look for the light, and exit. Once in the Lower World, follow your intuition as to which nature spirit you wish to visit.

When you are with this spirit, feel its energy and let this vibration fill you. You may ask questions or just soak up whatever you are feeling. If you are given suggestions about your life, remember this wisdom. Once the drum speeds up, thank this spirit of nature and say good-bye. Make your way to your starting place, take a few deep breaths, stretch, and open your eyes.

• •

Check-In

What was your Lower World like this time?

Which spirit of nature did you visit? Describe this spirit and your connection.

Did you receive any wisdom for your ordinary life?

• •

Travel through Water

I am a mermaid swimming through deep water in the cave, able to breathe and use my tail for speed and navigation. I pop my head out of the water and ask, "Which way to the dolphins?" A voice answers, "Straight down; dive and swim toward the light." The color of the water becomes purple and then a small glimmer of light appears. I swim into a grotto of ferns, then into a pool with a river of fresh water flowing to the sea. I sun myself on a rock, still a mermaid, with long hair, a fin instead of feet, and human hands. In

the distance I see dolphins coming, an entire pod with
a white one in the lead. I slide into the water, realize I
am now a dolphin, and the white dolphin and I com-
municate non-verbally with our eyes and spirits. We
swim side-by-side. I ask what to do with my life. He
tells me to keep my heart open no matter what.

The above water journey illustrates how amazing it is to become immersed in another world, in this case the world of water. And so, not only can you fly in the element of air or run on the earth as an animal, you can now swim like a fish! Water is its own teacher, too. It has taught me to relax, go with the flow, let myself be carried, to trust, and to become cleansed, renewed, and reborn on my return.

Not only have I been able to swim in the Lower World as a mermaid and a dolphin, but in the Middle and Upper Worlds, too. Very recently, when visiting my husband in a level of heaven, we decided to dive into the sea and become dolphins. We swam, played, had a jumping contest (we tied), and even swam to an underground palace. Water can be the conduit for some amazing spirit adventures as well as meaningful lessons.

Intention and Protection

The intention for this journey is to go to the Lower World and travel through a body of water. This might occur in the tunnel or after you exit. Just intend to have an experience of swimming underwater. For protection, just say what has worked previously.

Water Journey

As previously, begin the drumming recording and think of your intention. Once you arrive underground, follow your intuition about whether to find water here or to wait until you exit.

When you find a body of water, dive or jump in. Notice that you are perfectly safe and able to breathe easily underwater like a fish. Eventually, you will come up from this water world, and find yourself on land. This may still be in the cave or out in the light. Let the journey unfold from here and ask whatever questions you wish of the water, the land, or any beings you meet there.

When the drum speeds up, thank this world and its beings and say good-bye. Return the way you came, and when you are back at your starting place, take a few deep breaths, stretch, and open your eyes.

• •

Check-In

What experience did you have in water?

Did any animal helpers or spirit beings join you on this journey?

Did you receive any wisdom or have any realizations?

• •

Research

In addition to analyzing your journey on your own, it is enriching to do research on the Lower World, especially about your animal helpers. Earlier I recommended the book *Animal Speak*, but you can also research your animal online and find some of Ted Andrews' descriptions and other information about power animals. If, for instance, your animal helper is a bison, then just type "power animal, bison" into a search engine. This way you won't just get a description of the real animal.

Read about the mythological and historical background of your power animal, especially how this animal is symbolic and why he or she has cóme into your life. What I love most is to take a journey and interact with my animal helper. Then when I do research, often what I experienced in the journey is exactly what the literature presents. This confirms for me that the shamanic world is real, that it is rich with meaning, and that I can trust that I am on the right track.

· ·

Check-In

Do research on your animal helper or helpers from the Lower World and record your findings in your journal.

· ·

Real-Life Animals

Beginning to do journeywork will open your senses and your spirit to attracting animals, birds, reptiles, and insects in the real world. Ideally you are becoming more conscious and connected to everything around you.

Two days before my husband's death, I went for a walk by the ocean. As I was leaving the beach, a cobalt blue dragonfly flew directly in front of me, spun in circles, and danced up to the light and back to the earth. The dragonfly flew around me for some minutes and seemed intent on getting my attention.

Then, when I reached my car, I looked down and right by the door was a dead blue dragonfly, fully intact, but dried. I picked it up and took it home to put on my altar. Usually, I do research right away, but I just placed the dragonfly on my altar and returned to being my husband's caregiver. This was a Thursday, and my husband died on Saturday morning. Was the dragonfly trying to teach me about life and death, and hint that my husband was leaving soon?

After my husband's passing, I finally sat down and looked up the meaning of the dragonfly. When it appears, it is signaling a time of going into the light, or encouraging us to rise to the light, to the highest in our lives. My husband was going into the light, and I believe the dragonfly was trying to help me prepare for his passing, was reminding me that our spirits are of the light, and when no longer embodied, can be pure light.

I'm sharing this experience to encourage you to open your eyes and your heart to the natural world around you, where you can commune with all life, from rocks and shells to butterflies and lizards and coyotes; from hawks and owls to clouds and lightning. Begin today to notice everything with new vision.

. . . .

Check-In

What animals have you encountered in real life recently? Do some research on them, and then continue to write about animal encounters in your journal as they happen to you.

. . . .

Divination

Besides being aware of nature, begin communing with it. If you are walking down a busy street and a ladybug lands on your arm, you can silently ask the ladybug if it has a message, and then see if one comes into your mind. Then look up ladybugs later and see what the further meanings might be. If you hear a crow call, see if you can tell what it is saying. If you find a rock or shell, before taking it, ask if you can do so, and you will clearly hear a *yes* or a *no*. Every time you watch clouds float overhead, see if they have a message for you, or if you see a hawk on a wire or flying, again see if it has a message. Do this especially if a being comes into direct contact with you, as the dragonfly did with me. If a butterfly flies directly in front of you, commune with it and listen for a message in your mind.

Let your shamanic work open a lifelong connection to the world of nature, knowing you are part of the natural world and can find so much joy and self-discovery in this communion.

● ●

Check-In

Record any "conversations" with the natural world in your journal.

● ●

Insight *to* Action

What insights have you received in this chapter, and what action could you take to create a more fulfilling life?

Wrap Up

Now that you know how to journey to the Lower World and meet animal helpers, you can travel to this realm any time. Let yourself be guided by your senses, heart, and spirit rather than your mind. The more we journey, the more we can lighten up and even laugh at ourselves, and the spirit world has a sense of humor, too.

Recently, my son journeyed to find his horse, since he was born in the year of the horse. At first he says he felt proud of his muscular black horse. Then he looked at the horse from the front, and the horse's face looked just like the horse from the TV show *Mister Ed*, complete with huge teeth and a crazy grin. His message to my son: "Don't take yourself so seriously!" Each experience teaches us what we need to learn in that moment. Then the moment changes, we change, and our spirit travel changes, too. Just relax, have fun, and enjoy the ride.

⇐ 3 ⇒

Upward Travel

On my path I find a Great Tree
full of light and golden fruit;
and looking up see my husband
smooth-skinned with brown hair
curling to muscled shoulders.
He swings to the ground, picks
a bright globe, feeds me a bite
then eats the rest, pulp and juice
on lips and chins. Sticky with
sweetness, we laugh and kiss.
Pear shaped with mango seed,
the Chinese and Hindus
say these fruits bring
love, abundance
immortality.

—From my poem "Immortality"

The above poem describes my journey just two days before my husband's transition. He had never appeared in my journeys before, since it is usually spirit beings and departed loved ones that come. Only after his death did I understand the significance of this powerful encounter. The Great Tree in my journey is similar to the Tree of Life in the Bible and the Jewish Kabbalah, and many cultures describe such a tree as the giver of immortality. In the journey, my husband only gave me a bite of fruit because I am still embodied and it is not my time to die, but he ate the entire pear, representing his transition to a life of immortality.

Now that my husband is an immortal spirit, the Tree supports my access to him, to my soul family and divine teachers. More is said about how you can visit these worlds and their sacred spirits in the chapters that follow. A section of this chapter is devoted to this Great Tree, and you are invited to take a journey to find your own.

I walk through purple flowers, just enjoying their color and scent, when suddenly a large orange and yellow butterfly swoops down and tells me to get on. Right away I notice how soft her wings are, and I can see light through them, realizing these wings may have been the inspiration for stained glass windows. She tells me to be in the present moment and feel only joy. I focus even more on her softness and beauty, and when I do, I am completely in the present and feel deep happiness. Butterfly flies higher and higher and finally lands on a snowy mountain, and there at the pinnacle is a Russian palace.

Besides climbing the Great Tree, as shamans call it, you can journey to higher realms by climbing a magical ladder; you can also be carried by birds, flying horses, and other creatures such as insects and dragons. You may be lifted by wind, orbs of light, stars, angel beings, or by shape-shifting into a bird or soaring under your own power. The above journey illustrates how you can meet a helper like the butterfly to carry you to realms above. It doesn't matter that the butterfly is tiny; in the shamanic world you can ride on a butterfly's back! This chapter presents ways to travel upward, using several "vehicles," and perhaps your own unique "transportation."

- -

Check-In

What are some ways you have already traveled within the spirit worlds?

Have you shape-shifted into any being? Explain.

Have you traveled in or from your Middle World of personal power?

Do you have a tree that is prominent in your Middle World?

Have you ever traveled upward spontaneously during previous journeys? What happened?

- -

Travel from the Middle World

The best way I've found to travel to upper levels is through the Great Tree. Before taking such a journey it will help to understand the mystical and mythical importance of this Tree. My hope is that you will feel even greater respect for this wise teacher once you learn its history.

The Tree of Life

As I walk the dirt path through a meadow of flowers, my Tree of Life rises on a nearby hill. It is enormous, with spreading branches, green leaves, and golden fruit. From a distance it seems to take up most of the sky. This time there is something different about my tree, something that is grey on the trunk. As I reach the Tree, I see an elephant's head at the base, with bowed head and closed eyes. All is silent, so I start to climb as quietly as I can, carefully placing each foot on a limb. The branches move and seem to respond to my touch. I put my arms around the trunk as far as I can and lean my head on the smooth bark. I find myself asking, "What is your name?" and the Tree answers in my mind, "Ganesh." I remember that Ganesh is a Hindu god and the remover of obstacles. I thank Ganesh for being so welcoming and climb steadily to the top.

I didn't know during this journey that Ganesh would be a part of my Tree from this moment forward, or that he would be a sacred teacher, friend, and patient listener. Through doing research I now realize why Ganesh has come into my life, and why only his head appears. Ganesh's head symbolizes Atman, or the soul, and also represents wisdom, knowledge, education, success, and wealth. His body symbolizes Maya and this world, not the world of spirit, and thus, is not part of my Tree.[6] When you find your Tree, you may want to do research to discover the deeper significance of your encounter.

For over twenty years I have been blessed with a Tree of Life in each spirit world. In the Lower and Middle Worlds, the Trees provide a place for dialogue, and I often meet with my power animals and spirit allies in their branches. Also, I climb this sacred Tree in my place of power to get closer to the Upper World and facilitate my journeys there. Currently, the Tree of Life in my meadow of flowers is the greatest and most expressive one yet. This latest Tree, with its massive trunk and elephant head, provides access to all the upper realms, including a level of heaven.

A World View of the Tree of Life

Two writers have helped me understand the meanings surrounding the Tree of Life and Jacob's ladder: Rachel Pollack and Cherry Gilchrist. Pollack, in her book *The Kabbalah Tree*, presents a history of the Tree of Life from a cultural perspective. She begins with a discussion of Siberian shamanism and how the healers and shamans literally set up a pole, small tree, or ladder during the ceremony; then when they go into trance, they envision climbing to the spirit world to find a power object or to find how to heal a tribal member.[7]

In Cherry Gilchrist's book *Russian Magic: Living Folk Traditions of an Enchanted Landscape*, she presents what she terms the Cosmic Tree, and describes it as connecting the Lower, Middle, and Upper Worlds in Siberian shamanic practice. In their universe, a World Tree stands at the center, its branches stretching to heaven and its roots going into the earth, connecting the celestial and earthly realms. Gilchrist sees the Tree as a symbol representing the connection between God and human; it is a symbol of everlasting life or immortality, and it unites all of creation.

She further explains that such a Tree is the way shamans stay clear as to their direction, using the Tree as a highway between the worlds.[8] This is exactly how it feels when journeying through my own Tree of Life; I begin by climbing the tree, usually meeting an animal helper or spirit ally at the top and then traveling to the Upper Worlds, and I always return to the treetop and then climb down and back to ordinary reality. The Great Tree is a familiar bridge that facilitates safe spirit travel.

Besides the shamanic tradition, which is thousands of years old, there are also many references to the Great Tree in various religious traditions. Perhaps the greatest mention of the Tree of Life is in Jewish and Christian texts. In Jewish tradition, presented in the Kabbalah, the Tree is described with ten interconnected nodes and is drawn as a glyph of connecting circles and lines representing the levels of creation and a path toward spiritual awakening.[9]

In the Old Testament, beginning in Genesis, the Tree of Life is placed in the east of the Garden of Eden and is protected by angels and a flaming sword.[10] In the Book of Proverbs, the Tree is described as a golden crown covering the entire garden and four streams pour from its roots: milk, honey, wine, and oil.[11] In the Book of Enoch it is said that the chosen of God will eat the fruit from the Tree of Life.[12] If this is true, then I feel honored to have taken a bite, and honor my husband who ate the fruit down to its seed.

In the New Testament in the Book of Revelation, the Tree of Life is said to bear twelve fruits and yield one each month, and the leaves are for the healing of nations.[13] In the Catholic faith, the fruit of the Tree of Life is Christ himself, and in Eastern Orthodox Christianity the Tree of Life is said to be the love of God. Similarly, in Islamic tradition the Tree represents immortality.[14] This symbolism seems to come full-circle back to Siberian shamanism, and Gilchrist's view that the Great Tree represents immortality and our connection to the divine.

• •

Check-In

Have you ever had a connection with a special tree? Write about it in your journal.

Does anything in the above discussion about the Tree of Life resonate?

• •

Practice

As a child I practically lived in my pepper tree. I would lie on the wooden platform for hours, sometimes reading, but usually just looking at the wind in the wispy leaves and at the clouds moving across the sky. My tree was my castle, where I felt invincible, and where I connected with the spirits of nature and with angels. And so, even at a young age, my tree was the ladder I climbed to heaven. I've known this forever on some level, but right this moment it is clear that I needed (and perhaps we all do), a way to feel rooted in the earth and to being human, and still connected to something greater, whether it is the stars, the universe, a creative force, or God.

As weather permits, spend time outdoors, under, near, or in a tree. Yes, the best way to deeply experience a tree is by climbing it and sitting in its branches, if you can safely do so. Of course you need a large tree, a sturdy one, and preferably one that chooses you. By this I mean a tree that feels like the perfect one, the tree that literally seems to beckon to you, that your intuition says is the right one. Once you are with your tree, close your eyes and listen; perhaps see if the tree has a message for you or tells you its name. Touch its bark, its limbs and leaves, if they are present. Commune with your tree, and when you leave, thank it.

Check-In

Describe the tree you chose. Why did you choose this one?

What happened during the time you spent with your tree?

Did you receive any messages, wisdom, feelings, memories, or anything else?

Intention and Protection

Now it's time to find and climb your own Great Tree in your place of power in the Middle World, and perhaps take a spin into the upper realms. You will be journeying into the Upper Worlds in the next few chapters, so you can wait, or you can explore "up" if you wish. If you don't yet have a Tree in your sacred place, then you will first need to intend one into being when you first reach your place of power. You can just spend time with your Tree, remembering that it has a big spirit and can commune with you. For protection, just ask that you travel safely to your place of power to commune with your Tree and back again.

Great Tree Journey

Get ready to journey as you have before. Turn on the drumming recording and find yourself on your path to your personal place of power. As you look around, is there a Tree of Life or Great Tree in your place of power? Was it here previously, or did your intention create it this time? If there is no Tree, just intend that a Tree of Life appear that will facilitate your travel upward. The perfect Tree of Life will appear for you.

Once you see the Tree, walk to its base and look up. Touch its trunk and notice if it is bare or if it has any leaves and fruit. Everything is symbolic and important. You can begin a dialogue now, or wait until you are higher up. Begin climbing your Tree to the top and find a nice place to lean or sit. You may want to talk to your Tree at this point, or continue your conversation if it has already started. See if your Tree has a name and any information about its history, origins, or purpose in your life.

While at the top of your Great Tree, you can choose whether or not to stay there or take a whirl around the sky above the Tree. It's up to you. In other journeys in this chapter you will be able to soar into the worlds above your Tree.

When the drum speeds up, thank your Tree and begin your descent. Find yourself on your path and back to the world of ordinary reality. Open your eyes and recall as much detail as possible.

Check-In

What was your path and place of power like on this journey?

Did you already have a Tree of Life, or did you intend one to appear? Describe your Tree.

What transpired between you and your Tree? Recount any messages or wisdom.

Did you stay in your Tree or travel beyond?

Research

You might want to do research on such things as the type of tree in your place of power, the name of your Tree (if it shared its name), any message that has cultural, mythological, or mystical meanings, and so on. Just find out whatever you can about the Great Tree growing in your garden.

The Mystical Ladder

I walk through the gate to my garden as dusk falls, and pink light illumines my Great Tree. Its trunk is gnarled and there is a wooden door, polished and shining. The door at the bottom of the trunk looks inviting and I know if I open it, a soft chair, roaring fire, and a cat on a braided rug await me. But tonight I know I am to climb the stout branches to the top and travel to upper realms. The limbs are smooth and easy to climb, and I pull myself up to the very top. There I sit and watch the last rays of sun slide behind the hills, and the first stars appear faintly in the sky.

Before I can settle in too comfortably, a golden ladder comes tumbling down from above, end over end, until its bottom rung is level with the highest branch. It is a pliable ladder made of gold, not rope, but it swings like a rope ladder. I begin to step from rung to rung as the ladder swings in the sky and moves upward by some invisible force. Suddenly, the ladder is lifted up higher and higher until I no longer need to climb, and I find myself in billowing white clouds with just a glimpse of land above.

Such a ladder has appeared less frequently in the past few years, but early in my journeywork, a ladder was often my way of accessing the higher spirit worlds. The ladder always appeared in this manner, swinging in the sky and lifting me by invisible hands.

From childhood Sunday school I vaguely remember a song about climbing Jacob's ladder, yet I never did research when the ladder first appeared. It is now while writing this chapter that I discover this biblical story, and find it so parallel to my own experience. Even more parallel is the historical description of a ladder used by shamans to climb to the Upper World, which is thousands of years old, and older than the biblical story of Jacob. In indigenous communities, such as in Siberia, the shaman is a mediator between the tribe and the spirits, and will often build a ladder and actually climb it in demonstration to ensure the confidence of the community. Then the shaman goes into a trance, and while in an altered state will climb a mystical ladder, speak with spirits, and bring back wisdom for the tribe.

Similarly, climbing the ladder has brought me wisdom about my own life, and when I journey on behalf of others, I return with information for them. The ladder, then, is a vehicle, a bridge between this earthly world and the non-ordinary reality where the spirits of animals, family, allies, guides, and teachers help us to fulfill our purpose and assist others on their paths.

Jacob's Ladder

The Bible says in Genesis 28:12, "And he dreamed and behold a ladder set up on the earth and the top of it reached heaven and behold the angels of God ascending and descending on it." Before Jacob had his dream, he left after an argument with his brother and went into the wilderness alone. Jacob stops for the night in Luz and uses stones for his pillow. While he sleeps, Jacob has a vision. He sees a ladder on the ground that reaches up to heaven, and he also sees angels climbing up and down the ladder. The Hebrew meaning of the word angel is "messenger," and messengers are also the spirit allies that we meet on our shamanic journeys.

What is wonderful about the Great Tree and the mystical ladder is that they can be used to travel in both directions, and help create the perfect balance between heaven and earth. They remind me that we are both human and divine, having bodies and souls, living our time here until our bodies wither, but the essence of who we are lives on into eternity.

Jacob doesn't set up the ladder himself as shamans do, nor does he climb the ladder as I and shamans have done many times. In the Book of Genesis, 28:13, we learn why. Rather than climbing the ladder to God, God comes to Jacob. God says he will not leave Jacob and will help him and his descendants. Jacob is frightened by this visitation, but still makes an offering in a ceremony, taking the stone he has slept on and raising it as a pillar and anointing it with oil. He names the place Beth-el and calls it "God's house."[15]

This prophetic dream of Jacob's is similar to the visions of shamans who augment their power and bring back messages for the good of their people. In essence, this is the purpose of doing shamanic journeywork: learning how to listen to sacred teachings and using this wisdom to transform our lives and the lives of our fellows. How blessed we are that, like Jacob, we can alter the course of our lives while still living; we don't have to die to receive the blessings of heaven. All we have to do is be open to the spirit-messages meant for our evolution.

Check-In

Did you know the story of Jacob's ladder, or is it new to you? What are your thoughts about it?

What do you think about using a mystical ladder to climb upward?

Intention and Protection

The intention for this next journey is to go to your place of power and ask for a ladder to drop to you at the top of your tree. Then climb the ladder, perhaps to a first level of the Upper World, or just climb it and then return to the tree and your sacred place. For protection, just say whatever works for you.

Mystical Ladder Journey

Prepare for this journey as you have previously. Start the drumming recording and find yourself on your path to your sacred place in the Middle World, setting the intention of arriving in your place of power. Once at the top of the tree, look up and see a ladder unfurling all the way down to where you are. Notice what it looks like and get the feeling that you are to climb this ladder easily and safely. If it feels right, have a dialogue with the ladder. Why has it come and what does it hope you will experience?

Begin to climb the ladder, noting if you climb all the way up to the top or if something unseen helps you by lifting the ladder. By following your intuition, decide whether to climb up and back down or to explore a bit of the higher realms.

When your experience feels complete and the drum speeds up, begin making your way back to your path, and then back to the ordinary world. Take a few deep breaths and open your eyes.

Check-In

Where were you when the ladder unfurled, and what does your ladder look like?

If you engaged with your ladder, what did you talk about?

Where did you go when you climbed the ladder?

Did anything happen that merits research? Record your research in your journal.

Other Transportation Upward

I climb to the top of my Great Tree and White Winged One is waiting for me. He shape-shifts between an eagle and a swan, but more like a swan this time. We fly like a rocket to the sun.

~

Walking through the field of red poppies, I become a blue dragonfly and wing my way to the top of the tree. My Great Tree is covered in white flowers that smell like jasmine. Sunlight warms my face, and then as a dragonfly I soar first through starlight, then moonlight, and finally through the sun.

~

Snake crawls out of the water where he has been bask-
ing in the shallows, opens his wings, and tells me to hop
on. Together we fly to one of the first levels in the upper
world, a rocky island in the sky with a spiral path to a
high mountain.

~

I drop through thin air from the rock bridge, tumbling
over and over toward the canyon floor. Suddenly I am
caught by a masked super hero, not Superman, but
more comical like Snoopy dressed as the Red Baron!
He carries me to the moon in what looks like a plastic
hamster ball, and then to a level of heaven.

~

At the top of the Great Tree I am surprised to see my hus-
band Tom waiting for me. He is pleased he has surprised
me and immediately puts two fingers in his mouth, whis-
tles and yells, "Taxi!" A floating bubble of light appears,
a bit like Cinderella's coach, a door opens, and we get
into the backseat. The bubble taxi careens into the night.

As you can see, the spirits often are funny, and
when they come in such a way, I know it is time for
me to lighten up. These snapshots of my journeys are to
give you an idea of what might transport you upward. It
could be anything. I especially like it when a star or a
shaft of light beams down and picks me up. It is always
so magical. You will have a chance to travel with a few
of these helpers, and just know that ones that are not
mentioned here could also be your vehicles.

Now that you have found the Tree of Life and your ladder, it is time to invite in other beings to assist you in your flight. I use the word "flight" intentionally, as you will be flying, riding, jetting, whirling, spiraling, and in general rising and soaring to several worlds in the next few chapters.

Bird Helpers

If you have already met a bird as an animal helper in chapter 2, then this can be your first vehicle to higher levels, just as Eagle was and still is mine. Perhaps you have a hawk, eagle, condor, owl, swan, raven, vulture, hummingbird, or other bird as your totem. Then this may be the being that shows up to carry you skyward. If you don't currently have a bird as one of your power animals, then you can invite one to appear in the next journey. Having a bird as a power animal can help you travel to all the upper realms from your place of power or from your Great Tree. It's also exhilarating and magical to fly on their feathered backs to the worlds above.

Bird Mythology

You may have done research on a bird in chapter 2 if one appeared as your power animal. For those of you who did not meet a bird helper or do research, here are a few descriptions of birds and their symbolism.

The eagle is renowned as the king of the birds, is most closely associated with the Source or God. In Greek and Roman culture Zeus and Jupiter were associated with the eagle, and Zeus could change into an eagle at will. Perhaps the Greeks were already aware of shape-shifting, and Zeus was actually a shaman!

The eagle was often associated with mystical power to the Native Americans on this continent, and the Pueblo believe that the eagle can spiral upward until it passes through a hole in the sky to its home in the sun. Eagles symbolize nobility and divine spirit and those who have the eagle as a totem are being asked to bear great responsibility for their spiritual growth. Ted Andrews says that those with the eagle totem can "move between the worlds, touch all life with healing, and become the mediator and the bearer of new creative force within the world."[16]

The hawk is also a powerful totem, and Andrews calls them the messengers, protectors, and the visionaries of the air. Having a hawk as a power animal invites us to evolve to a higher consciousness. They also represent a higher awareness or psychic ability and skill in astral projection. Since shamanic journey is spirit travel, having the hawk as a power animal means being gifted at such travel. Because Hawk is so powerful as a totem, balance is required, and an ability to handle the intense life force of hawk medicine.[17]

Swan is a new animal helper for me, and often greets me at the top of the Great Tree. She is a feminine, gentle, and loving helper that carries me to a level of heaven. Swan alternates with Eagle, my masculine totem animal, and together they help balance my own masculine and feminine energies. In general, as a totem the swan awakens the emotions, and helps individuals become more sensitive and more aware of the feelings of others. According to Andrews, the swan is the totem of the child (within us), the poet, the mystic, and the dreamer.[18]

Check-In

Do you already have a bird as a totem? If so, what is it? Describe your bird. If not, is there a bird that resonates with you?

If a bird has already appeared in your Lower or Middle World, and you didn't do research, you can do it now and record any insights in your journal.

• •

Practice

In my own life, birds are very important soothsayers, and when they come near me, I notice, and either receive a message or do research on them. Recently, while in my backyard, I saw at least fifty pelicans flying above me in a giant circle, moving in and out of one another in an elaborate dance. They did this for about ten minutes, and just as they were leaving, a huge raven zoomed through my patio just above me. He didn't see me and was definitely on an important errand! A minute or two after this, a hummingbird flew to the last of the roses and drank deeply. I intend to do research on each of these birds and know that their symbolism is important.

This reminds me of a visit I had from a hummingbird years ago. I had the front door open and the sun was just coming up over the trees. I walked to the door and saw a hummingbird flapping its wings against the glass. Something told me to put out my finger like a twig and slowly move toward the bird. He landed on my finger, and then I carefully moved to the opening and he flew out into the light. In reading about hummingbirds, I found that they symbolize the finding of miracles and joy in any life situation.

From now on, be more aware of any birds that come near you, especially if they fly right in front of you or back and forth, or if they sit on a branch above or next to you. Also, be aware of birds that fly in front of your car, as owls and hawks tend to do. If you live in a city, you may need to go into the country or to a park where birds freely come. Look for birds on telephone lines or perched on buildings. Notice the birds around you and write down a description of them if they aren't ones you recognize. You might want to research the birds you see and discover what they symbolize, noting why they may have come into your life at this time.

Check-In

Write about the birds you've recently seen in your journal.

Record your research about the birds, especially their symbolic meanings.

Intention and Protection

Your intention for this journey is to travel to your place of power and climb your Tree or other high place. Then intend that a bird comes to carry you upward. This can just be a test flight, or your bird may wish to take you to a higher level. For protection just say what works for you.

Bird Journey

Get settled comfortably, relax, and begin the drumming recording. Envision yourself on your path to your place of power. As you have done previously, look for a higher place in your garden, perhaps a Great Tree or plateau. Climb to the top and spend some time communing with the world around you, perhaps having a conversation with the spirit of the Tree or high place.

Then look up and ask for a bird to fly down to meet you. Just let the bird that is meant for you arrive. When it lands, notice all its features. When you get the sense that you are to get on the bird, do so and fly with him or her. You can have a dialogue with your bird, and remember that this helper's words will come in your mind. Just follow your intuition about whether to fly nearby or go to a higher level. Sometimes your bird will help you make a decision.

When the drum speeds up, begin making your way back to your place of power, still being carried by your bird. Thank your helper and descend, making your way back to the path. When you are ready, open your eyes, take a breath, and record what you experienced.

Check-In

Did you speak with your Tree or high place? If so, what did you talk about?

Describe the bird that came to you.

If you communicated with your bird helper, what did you talk about?

Where did you go?

If you wish to do research on your bird, record it in your journal.

Other Winged Allies

You also might have a butterfly, dragonfly, bee, or other flying creature appear in your place of power. Of course, a flying horse, stag, dragon, or other mythical being could come to carry you, too, or even a flying human like a superhero! Any flying helper could offer you a ride, and the surprise is sometimes the best part.

In terms of mythology or symbolism, the butterfly, dragonfly, and bee all have rich histories. From my own experience riding on.their backs, the butterfly represents transformation and emergence for me, the dragonfly reflects the realms of light, and the bee sips the beauty and nectar of life, and reminds me that there is much to be savored. Whenever a butterfly comes into my shamanic or real life, it tends to be uplifting and joyful, letting me know that although change is inevitable, it can be sweet. The dragonfly, to me, represents immortality, as it soars higher and higher into the light of spirit. The bee teaches that we can enjoy our work and, with a kind of alchemy, turn flowers into honey, or our efforts into achievements. These totems are inspiring, carrying our spirits upward as we fly with them.

I have a white flying horse named Phoenix, have flown on a flying stag, and have been carried by a winged snake that insists he is not a dragon. In Greek mythology, the hero Bellerophon rides Pegasus in his defeat of the Chimera, but Bellerophon falls off his back. Zeus immortalizes the hero by placing him in the night sky in the constellation Pegasus.[19]

Winged snakes are found in the myths of many cultures, particularly in Asia and Central America, and were even present here in North America in the Anasazi, Zuni, Tiwa, and Hopi tribes. Only in Europe were winged serpents (dragons) vilified, and in Cambodia, China, and Egypt, the winged snake is thought to be a bringer of good fortune. It is often seen as a protector, especially of kings, queens, and other leaders, and in Egypt two winged snakes guard King Tut's tomb. One of the most famous winged serpents is Quetzalcoatl of the Toltecs, and later the Aztecs. This deity may have originated in Olmec culture as early as 900 BC, and his worship spread throughout Central America into the 1500s. Quetzalcoatl is thought to be a creation deity, patron of priests, and, some say, is related to fertility and rain.[20]

My own winged water snake was my protector, and he often wrapped himself around my shoulders for comfort or curled at my feet. He took me on many journeys and always guarded me and guaranteed safe passage.

Your own flying beings may be different from those described, but they will be perfect for you and offer you just what you need.

•••

Check-In

Is there a winged being besides a bird that feels special to you?

•••

Practice

For several days (or for the rest of your life) be aware of butterflies, moths, ladybugs, dragonflies, bees, or other flying beings in your world. When my husband and I lived in the mountains we had millions of ladybugs come each year, and an expert told us that our property was a ladybug mating area. The lovemaking energy was incredible, and ladybugs are said to bring good luck! Notice if you see the same flying beings day after day. They are trying to tell you something. What is it? Also, record any dreams, visions, or journeys you have already taken in which these flying messengers have come.

Just last night something new and extraordinary happened when I journeyed to the Upper World. I climbed to a high red mountain for the first time, and four spirit allies came with me. All around us were bees, swarms of bees encircling us as if in a cocoon or protective bubble, flying all the way to a level of heaven, then back again to the mountain. I am still sorting this journey out, and am doing research. What I know now is that the bees are asking for my help in exchange for assisting me. I have a hive in my backyard, and this is helpful, but I feel I need to become more informed and do more to save our bees.

Intention and Protection

For this journey, set the intention to fly on, with, or as another type of winged creature, whether it is an insect, a flying horse, a winged serpent, or a superhero. If you intend to shape-shift into a winged being and do your own flying, invite a spirit helper to fly with you. Your request could be, "Please let me safely fly from my place of power and back again. Thank you."

Winged Allies Journey

Prepare as you usually do, turn on the drumming recording and find yourself in trance and walking on your sacred path.

Move toward the high place in your natural world and climb to the top. Look up and intend that a winged being, different from a bird, arrive to carry you into the sky. Perhaps communicate with this helper and take in everything about him or her. You can also ask his or her name and whatever else you'd like to know. Decide with your helper whether to just fly around or visit a loftier level.

When the drum speeds up, make your way back to your place of power. Before climbing down be sure to thank this flying helper. Descend and walk on your path to the place you began. Take a few deep breaths, feel yourself coming back to the ordinary world, and open your eyes.

Check-In

Did you receive any wisdom from your Tree or high place?

What flying helper arrived? Describe everything about this being.

What was communicated between you?

Where did you go and what happened there?

Record any research on this flying helper.

Other Transportation

At times it is not a being that carries us, but an object, like a bubble of light, or perhaps a star or dandelion fluff, or even a golden string that pulls us through the cosmos. On many occasions, a star has beamed down near me. I step into the beam and it flashes through the sky to the Upper World. I have also traveled inside a seed, a spiral of light, a tornado or cyclone, a rocket ship, and, as shared previously, a taxi bubble! One of my colleagues has a magic elevator that she takes up to the Upper World and down to the lower ones. The first time it appeared, an invisible presence said, "Going up?" The spirit world continues to surprise and delight with its offbeat humor.

Rather than thinking about an object to travel in, why not just let the magic happen? Whatever shows up to carry you will be just right. At times, letting go of outcome and letting your intention be more general allows the universe to give you exactly what you need, and something better than you could envision.

Intention and Protection

The purpose of this journey is to experience spirit travel inside an object, and also to practice letting go of outcome. You can ask that you are safely carried into the sky and back again.

Journey with Other Transportation

Just settle in, start the drumming recording, go into trance, and see yourself on the path to your place of power. Once in your natural world, begin to climb to the highest level, all the way to the top, and ask for an object to arrive. When something appears, notice what it looks like. Follow your intuition and the object's invitation, and then let it carry you into the sky. Again, either zoom around above your natural world or go to a higher level, whichever feels right.

You may or may not communicate with your object, but if you do, ask any questions you wish, or just receive information and wisdom. When the drum speeds up, come back the way you went, thank your helper, and climb down and back onto your path. When you are ready, open your eyes and record what happened.

Check-In

What came to carry you this time? Describe the object in detail.

What was communicated between you, if anything?

Where did you go and what happened there?

Your Own Power

As mentioned previously, it is best to travel on, in, or with a flying animal helper or spirit ally when traveling upward, especially once you journey through the sun to a level of heaven, as you will in the next chapters.

As you become more experienced, it is fine to fly with a human spirit being, such as an ally, teacher, or guide, or fly under your own power, and yet, after twenty years, I still travel on, in, or with a spirit ally. My guide Rama has flown with me many times, often holding my hand. You, too, may have a guide that can carry you, hold your hand, or fly beside you. Just know that this ally has been assigned to you and will be of service. Flying with a helper is not just for protection, but for the companionship and teaching that we can receive. More and more I realize that I don't have to do this work or this life alone. I can count on an infinite number of beings that love me and are waiting to offer guidance.

Now I am inviting you to spirit travel as yourself under your own power, but ask that you go with a helper. This could be an animal or a human spirit ally, a teacher, or a guide. If you wish, you can shape-shift into a being and fly into the sky. Perhaps you will become a bird, a flying horse, an insect, a winged snake, or some other flying helper not presented here. You can shape-shift into any being, but let a helper fly alongside. Also, you can fly as yourself, with your own ability to soar, whether with wings, jet propulsion, or some other means that is a mystery at this time.

· ·

Check-In

What comes up for you when thinking about flying on your own, either as a winged creature or as yourself?

Do you need to do anything to feel more comfortable on this journey? You can always hold a stone, light a candle, or, once in trance, invite a spirit ally to join you.

· ·

Intention and Protection

The purpose of this journey is to see how it feels to soar upward under your own power. In chapter 2, you were invited to shape-shift into an animal helper, and now you are being asked to shape-shift into a flying being, or to fly on your own, remembering that a helping spirit should accompany you. For protection, say whatever feels right.

Journey Using Your Own Power

Get comfortable and start your drumming recording. Go into trance and find yourself on your sacred path to your place of power. Climb to the highest point and see if your Tree or high place wants to communicate with you.

Once at the top, intend to either shape-shift into a winged being, or know you have the power to fly on your own. Invite in a helper to fly with you, or this being may have already arrived. You may want to ask questions of your ally, you may receive wisdom from them, or you could travel in silence, just enjoying the flight. See if you just travel above your place of power, or if you journey to an upper level.

When the drum speeds up, return the way you came, land in your high place, and walk down to your path. When ready, open your eyes, take a few deep breaths, and return to ordinary reality.

Check-In

Is there anything different in your natural world?
Did you find any metaphors or symbols?

Did you shape-shift or just use your own power?
If you shape-shifted, what did you become? If you
remained yourself, how were you able to fly?

Who or what arrived to fly with you? Describe your
spirit ally.

Describe what happened on this flight.

Insight *to* Action

After reviewing the above journeys and your
insights, what action would you like to take in
your real life?

Up, Up, and Away

Learning how to travel upward now gives you the foundation for the chapters that follow. You now have a Great Tree or high place, a mystical ladder, and helpers to carry you to the Upper World. From now on you can also fly on your own, either by shape-shifting or as yourself, and spirit allies can fly alongside. Only a few travel methods were shared, and the ways to spirit travel are infinite. May you let your journeys to higher realms unfold magically, trusting that the beings that love you are thrilled to soar by your side. Fly into sunsets and through the Milky Way, over the moon bridge and through the sun to worlds of light and reunion.

≈ 4 ≈

Stars, Moon, and Sun

Looking up at the stars at night,
filling up with clear white light,
greater than I was before,
their beauty makes me soar.

Not just solid, we're made of light;
more than bodies, we're sky at night;
a million stars and their energy
fill you and fill me.

There's Orion, and red Mars,
the Pleiades, all seven stars
remind me of what life is for
to know we're so much more.

God is in us too.
Every cell is born anew.
We're human, and we are divine.
Our mission is to shine.

—From my song "The Infinite"

I am a condor flying on wide wings over red canyons and across a star-filled sky. As I soar higher and higher, I become a ball of light and then a firefly, and rise up among the stars, landing on the Pleiades as myself. I enter a white stone building and walk down spiral stairs, torch in hand. A door appears and I step through into a room filled with blinding light.

A voice comes from the light and tells me to sit in the center, saying, "Eat the light, breathe it, let it fill your eyes, your ears, enter the top of your head and travel to the bottoms of your feet. Keep yourself filled with the spirit of light. Surround yourself with more light, for you are a star being and your essence is light. Shine forth in the world as a beacon to others. Remember who you are." I am completely filled with light and surrounded by light. I am light.

Isn't this the purpose of shamanic journeywork, to find out who we are at the deepest level, and then live our vision here on the planet? It is my belief, as I say in the above song, that our mission is to shine, by discovering our gift, our calling, and then become the person we are meant to be, and do what we are meant to do.

After this powerful journey to the Pleiades, a song sang itself in my head and became the final one on my CD *We Carry the Light*: "I'm a being of light, a bearer of light, a bringer of light, I am. Let my mission unfold, I am ready."

Check-In

At this point in your own journey, who are you and who do you want to become? Where are you now, and where do you want to be? You can focus on your personal or professional life, or on anything that feels important.

In my case, saying I am a light worker or a bringer of light and love is certainly not a heading in the phone book or at the top of my résumé! However, this is who I am. Who you are may also be more abstract and not defined by the usual terms. It is my hope that the previous and following chapters are helping you realize more about yourself and your purpose.

Rising Upward

In this chapter we continue the process of rising upward toward a level of heaven. All of the experiences in previous chapters will now assist you to travel up to the stars and moon, and experience the sun's energy. As you read in the above journey, I have flown to the star nation as a condor, as a ball of light, and then as a firefly. In other journeys to the stars, I have been a golden arrow, I have flown on wings of light, I have climbed steps of stars, and I have even become a star. Here is a verse of a song that came to me on a star journey:

Winging my way through time and space
Filling with wonder, joy, and grace.
Knowing what's true, we're not alone;
Surrounded by stars, we are home.

—From my song "Made of Stars"

Perhaps you will feel as supported as I do, and discover that we are not alone, not here on earth, with people and nature around us, and not in the spirit worlds either. It is a false belief that our egos tell us, that we are separate, isolated, and abandoned. Nothing could be further from the truth. We are loved by beings on earth and beyond, we are supported by nature, and this includes infinite constellations, the mystical moon, and an energetic sun.

Purpose of Star, Moon, and Sun Journeys

Traveling to the stars, moon, and sun can help you acclimate to the upper realms and reach a level of heaven. Many shamanic teachers say that the moon and stars are part of the Middle World, are part of our dreamscape and closest to our real life in ordinary reality. However, as will be explored in this chapter, I believe the moon, stars, and sun are gateways to the Upper Worlds, and have many of the characteristics of non-ordinary reality in the higher realms. In visiting stars for many years, I have found a divine presence and the same light that I've seen and felt in a level of heaven.

Perhaps more importantly, journeys to stars, moon, and sun may offer deep wisdom from seen and unseen beings, and you can return feeling motivated to live your life more expansively and authentically. Each time I journey into the sky, I fill with light. I often receive healings, blessings, or messages of encouragement and empowerment. I return feeling more confident and healed.

In this chapter you choose a star or planet that resonates, that somehow inspires you or even feels familiar. For many years I have felt an affinity with the Pleiades, so much so that my husband put this constellation on the ceiling above our bed. It glows in the dark and I can look at it and smile as I drift off to sleep. For many years, and even now, I search the night sky for the seven sisters every chance I get, and have the sense that I am a star being, not an earthling. I'm being very transparent with you in saying this, and I hope you don't think I'm delusional. My husband once teased me when I said, "I'm not from Earth," by adding, "You're not telling everyone this, are you?" Well, now I've told you, and my secret is out!

Here in this chapter you can journey to a star or planet of your choosing, or just let the destination be a mystery until you arrive. Perhaps you feel an affinity for a certain star or planet, or for the moon itself, as I do, and may feel at home as you visit the star nation.

Stars and Planets

The following is by no means representative of all the constellations in our universe, but these stars and planets are the best known in terms of cultural history, myth, and allegorical meaning. As you read about them, see if one especially interests you. As mentioned previously, you can also wait and see where you go.

Astronomers have recognized eighty-eight constellations in the sky in the northern and southern hemispheres. Researchers believe the very first civilizations to identify constellations were the Sumerians and Babylonians, and then their knowledge traveled to Egypt and Greece.[21] We know that the ancient Greek tradition was to name stars within constellations based on their shape, or to name them after gods, animals, and heroes.

My father taught me the constellations, and I have some favorites. The Big Dipper, for example, is part of a larger constellation called Ursa Major, or the Great Bear. There's also the Little Dipper or Ursa Minor, The Little Bear. Other familiar constellations are Orion, Cassiopeia, Cepheus, Draco, and Castor and Pollux. Perhaps you are interested in two of the brightest stars we see in the night sky, Sirius and Arcturus. You may be drawn to one or more stars, and can do more research on their history and mythology. Most star names come from Greek or Arabic words, and the mythology is often fascinating. It's also fun to do a journey first, noticing everything you can about the star or planet you visit, and then do research and find the name. This happened to a woman in my journey circle, who had a feeling she had reached Saturn and saw it was mostly gaseous and had moons or asteroids around it. Then when she did research, she found that her experience clearly described Saturn.

The constellation that has tremendous history and myth surrounding it, and even has a car company named after it (Subaru), is the Pleiades. The word "subaru" is Japanese for "gathered together," and is the Japanese word for the Pleiades. It's ironic that I drive a Subaru and didn't know this background when I bought it. No wonder I love my car! This constellation is one of the brightest in the night sky, and many myths exist about its formation and even why the seventh star seems to be missing. If the Pleiades intrigues you, go ahead and research all the myths and history of this constellation.

Perhaps you wish to visit a planet instead. Another participant in a journey circle decided to go to Venus, and then she and an army of spirit allies rode horses to the sun. Leading this army was Athena, Goddess of Wisdom, and many Greek archetypes were present in her journey. You can travel to Venus, Mercury, Mars, Jupiter, Saturn, Uranus, Neptune, and Pluto. You can also travel to one of the dwarf planets or a planet not in our solar system.

A psychic once told me I am from the planet Virgo, and this didn't resonate with me. But I researched Virgo and found that it is actually the second-largest constellation, is 260 light-years away, and includes a very bright, giant blue star near the bottom of the Big Dipper called Spica. There are a thousand galaxies in the Virgo cluster, so who knows, perhaps I am originally from one of them![22]

* *

Check-In

Are there stars or planets that you feel curious about? Write down their names.

You can also do research on these constellations and planets and write what you find in your journal.

* *

Practice

Go outside on a clear night with the intention of scanning the sky, connecting with the stars, and seeing which ones you can identify from prior knowledge or current research. Feel the vastness, and yet also the protective feeling of a bowl of light above you. Now look at the moon and notice if it is waxing or waning, new or full, or something in between. Stare at the moon and breathe in its light. Afterward, write about your experience with the moon and stars, especially if you found a star that calls you.

Star or Planetary Beings

> I journey on wings of light and soon come to stars that are steps up to the Pleiades. Once on the star I see a throne of light. Arianrhod, the Celtic Goddess of destiny and the moon is seated there, dressed in white and silver. I sit at her feet and she says: "Daughter, you are on the right path; your process is now being accelerated. You are birthing work that will be with you for the next thirty years. You are a being of light that is to share knowledge and love with everyone you meet. Come out of the darkness and reveal your light and power."

Many of my journeys to the moon and stars involve meetings with Arianrhod, who, after twenty years, is still one of my primary spirit teachers both in my place of power and in the realm of moon and stars. You may also have a special spirit being or archetypal figure that is your teacher. As you travel to a star or planet, and later to the moon, be aware of any being that speaks to you or that you see. Remember their appearance, their voice, and their words.

If you do research before you journey to a star or planet, you will find many archetypes, including gods and goddesses from ancient times associated with the sky realm. For instance, every constellation has Greek and Roman gods, goddesses, or heroes and heroines as part of its mythology, and you might encounter Zeus, Hera, Aphrodite, Athena, Apollo, Artemis, Poseidon, Demeter, and other gods, as well as Hercules, Orion, Jason, Theseus, Ganymede, Astraea, and other heroic figures.

The star being that appears to you may be from another cultural mythology too, such as Arianrhod who comes from the Celtic tradition. If you can't tell who it is and they don't say a name, you will have to take cues from their dress, manner, and message. This is how I discovered Arianrhod's identity. The discovery process is actually very rewarding and lends deeper meaning to your process.

Intention and Protection

Your intention for this journey is to travel to a star or planet other than the moon or sun. You will have a chance to journey to the moon later. In another chapter we travel through the sun's force field to get to a level of heaven.

Your intention is also to connect with the energy of this star or planet since you may not see anyone. On my star journeys, I usually do not see anyone, but I am surrounded by light and hear voices. Once I sat in front of a white throne and it seemed like a long time with nothing happening. Suddenly, the throne moved and shifted, and I jumped. A voice said, "I've been here all along, but you just couldn't see me."

Say whatever feels right in terms of protection. You can also hold a sacred stone or object for more grounding.

Journey to a Star or Planet

Begin the drumming recording, see your path, and walk to your place of power. Set the intention that it is night, but that you can see perfectly well. Once you arrive in this sacred place, immediately look for a way up. Perhaps you will see a tree, plateau, mountain, waterfall, or other high place.

Once you have reached the top, intend that a helper or object come to carry you to a star or planet. Get on, in, or fly next to a helper and begin your ascent into the night sky. Do not use your mind, but let your subconscious, your senses, and your emotions lead you.

As soon you arrive on a star or planet, begin to explore. Follow your intuition about where to walk, and use all your senses to discover as much as you can. Notice the surface of the star or planet, look around at the surroundings, and take everything in. Allow yourself to just follow what feels right, and you may find stairs to climb or descend. Remember your intention is to connect with the spirits of this place, to ask them questions, perhaps, or just to listen to them.

If you encounter a being or beings, be very present and take in all they communicate with you. If you can see them, remember their appearance and the energy you feel when with them. If they are invisible, just sense their energy and hear their words.

When the drum begins its call back, say good-bye and thank you and come back the way you came. Find your helper waiting and travel back to your place of power together. Climb down and walk along your path to the place you began. Take a breath or two, and, when ready, open your eyes.

. . . .

Check-In

Describe how you traveled to the night sky.

Did you go to a star or a planet? What did it look like? Do you know its name?

What happened while on the planet or star?

Overall, what is the feeling, sense, or message that is the most important one for you and your life at this moment?

If you do research on the star or planet, what do you discover?

. . . .

Becoming a Star

Besides traveling to a star or planet, you may actually become a star! This is what happened to me:

I am a firefly, flitting happily over the bridge, through the gate, and into my garden, then up to the top of my tree. Now as a woman, I see and feel pulsing light at my heart. Just then, a star shoots right into my heart and

I burst into a million bits of light that swirl and fly into the sky; then I come together as a new star. As a star, I glow and pulse in the night sky, and I ask for someone to come and teach me about being a star. A woman appears with a halo of golden light all around her shoulders and head. She tells me to feel the energy in my body, and teaches me a circular breathing technique to increase my energy. She gives me a cup of pure golden liquid to drink, and I feel this elixir pulsing through my body. Before doing healing work with my clients, she tells me to imagine drinking this light and holding my hands in star fire. When I hug her and say good-bye, I feel electric energy flowing through all my chakras. Finally, I come back to my sacred place as a beam of starlight, then become a firefly and fly out of the garden.

Journey Again

If you chose to travel to a star, then you might want to do another journey to a planet, or if you traveled to a planet, then journey to a constellation this time. Just follow the directions in the above section, including the questions to answer afterward. In this way, you are able to savor more of the night sky and connect with the beings that reflect this realm. Also, you might want to set the intention of becoming a star in your next journey.

After your journey, write about it in your journal, noting how you traveled there, where you went, and what happened, including any connections you made with star and planetary beings.

The Moon

*I am standing in a circle of torches, with my helpers
around me in love and protection. I look up as a star
comes toward me at great speed and picks me up. I
find myself inside this object of light. We fly to the
Pleiades, where I walk through door after door and
then out onto a balcony. Looking at the galaxy of stars
and full white moon, a bridge of light appears from the
moon and I cross over into luminosity. The Goddess
Arianrhod appears shimmering in white and silver and
says, "Your book is being channeled from me, from
your spirit allies, from the goddesses, from your past
selves in other lives, through you and into print. From
now on, every time you look at the moon, think of all
your support, and also know that you are connecting
with humanity everywhere."*

Re-reading these words has me in tears, feeling so
grateful and humbled by my spirit guide and by the gift of
this shamanic work. This powerful journey to the moon
has helped me to forge ahead in my life, trusting that
all is well and everything is unfolding for my highest.
Traveling to the moon from your place of power or even
from your star can assist you to connect with beings that
want to support you to become your greatest and most
evolved self. In my experience, these beings are often
goddesses and gods from various cultures, heroes and
archetypal beings representing kings, queens, teachers,
gurus, and other spirit allies.

Moon Lore and Mythical Beings

The moon is about 239,000 miles away, and over 2,000 miles in diameter, and the moon is usually said to be 4.5 billion years old. One scientific theory states that the young earth had no moon; a rogue planet hit the earth, and the resultant chunks of planet and the vaporous clouds that rose eventually condensed and joined other solid particles into what is now our moon. We know a great deal about the moon at this time, but ancient peoples created myths to explain the presence of the luminous moon and its phases.

The ancient Chinese believed there were twelve moons, one for each month of the year, and that the moons were made of water and had a white hare or a toad living in them. At the beginning of each month, the moon mother, Heng-O, washed her children in a lake at the western side of the world. Each moon, one child after the other would travel in a chariot for a month to reach the eastern side of the earth. This was how the Chinese explained month-long moon cycles.

Native Americans, especially the Algonquian peoples of the northeast, had many names for the full moon, and European settlers adopted these names when arriving in America. These names for the moon came from nature: the seasons, acts of hunting and fishing, and some farming. To illustrate, January is called "Wolf Moon" because of the hungry packs of wolves they heard howling in the night. February is called "Snow Moon" for the heavy snowfalls in the winter. March is termed "Worm Moon" due to all the earthworms available to the spring birds. April is called "Pink Moon" after an early blooming flower called moss pink. June is "Strawberry Moon."

Perhaps the name that is used by many Western peoples is "Harvest Moon," rising in September and reflecting a time when farmers can pick their crops later in the day by the light of the moon.[23]

In Hindu mythology, Soma is the moon god and also the name of a magical elixir that only the gods can drink. Hindus believed that this white potion was stored in the moon, and the more the gods drank, the more the moon would shrink. This explained the changing size and cycles of the moon. Like the Chinese, the Hindus thought that the moon was inhabited by a white hare, and thus all hares are seen as incarnations of the god Soma.[24]

Celtic cultures have several important goddesses, and the moon goddess Arianrhod is one of the most intriguing. Arianrhod means "silver circle," and I have seen her on a throne in the star realm with stars in a circle all around her. She has also been called High Fruitful Mother, Star Goddess, Sky Goddess, Goddess of Reincarnation, and Full Moon Goddess. She is still honored in some circles at the full moon and represents beauty and fertility as well. It is said that she is the goddess to invoke when women want to find their own power.[25] She has definitely done this for me.

Artemis (Diana to the Romans) was the Greek goddess of the moon and the hunt. The Greeks and Romans literally believed this goddess was the moon. Another Greek goddess, Selene, was the personification of the moon, and often wore a crescent moon and was pictured driving a chariot through the sky. Her Roman name was Luna and words such as lunar, lunacy, and lunatic come from her name. From the fifth century in Greece, people have attributed insane behavior to the time of the full moon.[26] The moon still invokes awe in most of us, and individuals and groups still do ceremonies at the new and full moon to honor her light and power.

●●●

Check-In

What have been your experiences with the moon?

Do any of the myths or archetypal beings just described interest you?

●●●

Practice

Plan to spend time at night looking at the moon in its phases, especially the new moon and full moon. Wishing on a new moon is an ancient practice, as this moon represents a new beginning or a chance to manifest your desire. The full moon is about fruition, abundance, sensuality, and fulfillment, and can be a time of gratitude and celebration for all your blessings.

After spending time looking at the moon, describe your feelings or thoughts in your journal.

Intention and Protection

Your intention is to travel to your Middle World and then journey to the moon and connect with one or more beings there. Your purpose is to ask for wisdom, or to ask questions about your life.

You can ask for protection as you have done previously, using the language that works best for you.

Journey to the Moon

How exciting. You are going to the moon, and you don't even need a spacesuit. You are a different kind of astronaut; all you need is your own intuition and your ability to go into a shamanic trance and allow the experience to unfold naturally. By now you know what works best for you in order to journey.

When the drumming starts, find yourself in your place of power. Now, as you did in the journey to a star or planet, look for a way up.

Climb to the top or find yourself there by another means. Set the intention that transportation will appear, and whatever comes is perfect.

Now travel with the intention of reaching the moon. Try to remember what you pass as you travel, and where the moon appears so you can record this later. Once you see the moon's light, begin your landing with the intention of exploring and eventually meeting a being that wants to connect with you.

Trust your intuition and walk in the direction that feels right. Soon a being will appear, or you will hear a voice or feel an energy or presence. Take in what you hear or sense. Ask questions about your life or just listen. Once the drumming speeds up, know that it is time to come back. Thank your helper and go back the same way you came.

Once you are back in your Middle World, you can walk to wherever your journeys begin. Return to ordinary reality, stretch, take a few deep breaths, and open your eyes.

Check-In

How did you travel to the moon? What did you notice while on your way?

How did the moon appear to you?

Did a spirit being meet you there? If so, record what happened between you.

Did any important insights come to you from this moon journey?

Is there any research you would like to do? Record your findings in your journal.

The Sun

As Swan carries me upward into the star-filled sky, I revel in the beauty around me, feel the soft downy feathers against my cheek, and sit up to see the moon rushing by on my right. We have been flying steadily and smoothly, when all of a sudden we hit something like a rubber barrier, an energy that is thicker, more solid and spongy. Swan flies into this force, her wings drawing back and her head pushing against the force field. We are traveling through the sun, and as we finally exit, we are "spit out" into the sky on our way to a level of heaven.

The above journey describes the way the sun's energy feels to me—dense, and as if it stretches as I pass through. It may seem different to you, but most of my workshop participants describe this viscous and stretchy energy field. I have never had a problem traveling through the sun's energy, but it is different from any other place in the spirit worlds. What is important for shamanic journeying is that the sun is the main force field we must pass through to get to the highest upper worlds, including a level of heaven.

Sun Worship and Myths

The sun is not worshiped today as it was in ancient times, and yet it still holds fascination for us and is still being studied by modern scientists. NASA studies the sun because of its effect on the earth in terms of solar flares and radiation, and watches it carefully for any changes that could affect our planet. NASA calls the sun "our home star," and describes it as a "seething, rolling ball of hot gasses that goes through cycles of quiet and violent outbursts."[27] It is the violent outbursts that concern scientists, even though these eruptions do not endanger us at this time.

We cannot visit the sun as we can the moon and stars, and this fact in ordinary reality is also true in shamanic work, as we discuss later in the chapter. The sun still inspires us, makes us feel alive and energetic, and infuses us with Vitamin D. Also, we can learn about the sun's history and better appreciate its gifts.

Nearly every ancient culture worshipped the sun as the giver of life and light and named its gods and goddess as the sun itself or keepers of the sun. In Egypt, the god Ra traveled through the sky in his solar boat, and barges were the usual means of travel for sun gods and goddesses prior to the second millennium. Ra was said to travel by barge in an underground passage from west to east so he could then rise in the sky at dawn. Ra would ride in his boat and drive away the demon Apep of darkness and make sure the world had enough light. During the Egyptian pharaoh Akhenaten's reign, Aten became the single god worshipped at that time and was represented by a disk of the sun.[28]

In the second millennium, when the chariot was invented, Greek, Roman, Norse, German, and Hindu deities often traveled in a chariot drawn by horses across the sky. The Greek Titan gods called the sun Helios, who wore a crown and rode a chariot through the bright sky. Later, the Greeks named Apollo the sun god, bringer of light. In Norse mythology the goddess Sol rode in her chariot, and in German myth both Sol and the goddess Sunna rode through the sky in chariots. The Hindus believed the sun was a king who rode through the sky in a chariot drawn by seven horses.[29] These cultures and others had such similar beliefs that it is clear that they all sought to explain the rotation of the sun from day to night and back to day in a way that helped them understand their world and feel safer in it.

One of the Aztec sun gods was Tonatiuh. The Aztec and Maya civilizations used the sun for the basis of their calendars and for many of their rituals and temple designs. The Aztecs also believed that if they did not practice human sacrifice, the sun god would not move across the sky, and everyone would perish. Many other cultures expressed fear about the sun, as in the story of Icarus, who flew too close to the sun and it melted his wings as he plummeted to earth. This story reminds us of how powerful the sun is, and that we must respect it.

Mythology about our sun helps us value its importance as life-giver, and perhaps reading the above stories reminds us that without our sun, the earth and humanity would perish. Shamanic work is so healing because like ancient peoples, we can now honor the sun as we travel through it to higher realms, and perhaps do some repair work on the ozone layer in the process! Finally, the sun is a powerful portal and will facilitate our passage to a level of heaven.

Check-In

What are your experiences with and feelings about the sun?

Do any of the cultural myths or deities resonate with you?

Do you have any nervousness about traveling through the sun's energy?

Practice

The next time you are outdoors on a sunny day, or even on a cloudy one, notice everything you can about the sun: its light, its warmth, what it does for nature and humans, and then write about your experience and insights.

Intention and Protection

The intention for this journey is not to actually go to the sun, which I have never done in twenty years, but to learn how to pass through the sun's energy or force field to higher realms. The sun, from my experience, is not a destination but a portal. My clients and workshop participants that have tried to travel to the sun were unable to do so due to the noise, the force field, or the heat. The sun, however, is the way to journey to the upper worlds.

The intention for this journey, then, is to travel through the sun's energy field, then back again to your place of power in the Middle World. For me, passing through the sun's membrane is a bit like being born. You move through the thick substance and pop out the other side. At least this has been my experience, and yours could be different. What is important is that you are not landing on the sun as you did in your star and moon journeys; you are passing through a field of energy that extends out from the sun. Just notice your way through.

Also, you may see other realms and feel curious about them, but save your exploration for the later journeys to the Upper World. You will get to a level of heaven in the next chapters.

The sun, according to shamans, is also the portal for souls crossing from the earth realm to the spirit world. Since we are still embodied and need to come back here to fulfill the rest of our purpose, it is important to say a protection prayer or affirmation, and it is suggested that you travel with or on a spirit being or animal helper. I have never traveled through the sun's energy alone.

A possible request could be: "I ask to safely travel through the sun's energy and back again. Thank you." If you wish, you can hold a stone, light a candle, and invite spirit beings to travel with you through the sun.

● ●

Check-In

Are any feelings coming up about this journey to the sun?

● ●

Journey to the Sun

Be clear about your intention and say your protection statement. Let the drum take you into trance and find yourself on the way to your sacred place of power. Once there, look for a way up: a tree, plateau, mountain, or other way to "climb" upward. Once at the top, intend for a being that loves you to come and accompany you or carry you to the sun.

Travel on, in, or with this being or force, knowing that you are perfectly safe with this guardian that protects you completely.

Move toward the sun, noticing what levels or worlds you pass in the process. Once you are close to the sun's energy, you will see intense light, you may hear a sound, and you may feel the force field before you arrive.

Following your intuition and that of your travel companion, move through the field of energy. Notice how it feels, and just keep intending to move through it to the other side. Be aware of how it feels or even sounds when you exit. Once out of the sun's field, you can fly around a bit and notice what is ahead. You are now in a much higher realm and on the way to a level of heaven.

After flying around and noticing what this higher level is like, it's time to come back. This, in a sense, has been an exploratory journey to show you how to reach the very highest realms we can access as embodied humans. You will need the ability to travel through the sun's energy in the chapters that follow.

When the drumming speeds up, make your way back to your place of power. Intend to land where you began in your place of power and find your way to the starting place on your path. Take some deep breaths, intend to remember all you experienced, and open your eyes.

• •

Check-In

What being or force of nature appeared to help you travel to the sun?

Describe your trip to the sun's energy field.

Once you reached the sun, how did it look, feel, or sound to you?

How did it feel to travel through the sun's energy?

What did you see or experience "on the other side of the sun"?

Did you explore any of these higher levels?

••

Insight *to* Action

What action can you take in your real life based on the wisdom received in this chapter?

Return from Space

In this chapter you have been an astronaut in a sense, traveling to stars, planets, the moon, and the sun, but unlike our own astronauts, you have journeyed farther and to realms they have never explored. You are a shamanic pioneer, a cosmic voyager, and you have brought back treasures as ancient explorers have done. Your gold, jewels, and moon rocks are the gifts of greater consciousness, self-knowledge, transformation, and the realization of your life purpose. Don't put away your wings yet. Get ready to fly to higher realms, including many of the upper worlds such as a level of heaven, to visit your soul family, sacred teachers, and loved ones. It's onward and upward from here.

⤶ 5 ⤷

Higher Realms

Be a spiral of light rising upward.
Let yourself . . . fly.
Be a spiral of light rising upward.
Feel yourself . . . be the sky.
Be a spiral of light rising upward.
Let yourself . . . soar high.

Spiraling, spiraling
deeper and higher,
higher and deeper
ever spiraling;
spiraling, spiraling
deeper and higher,
ever spiraling . . . home.

—From my song "Spiraling Home"

*A golden ladder drops from the sky and seems to be my
invitation to climb to a higher world. I just hold on and
let myself be lifted. I see clouds above me, and then the
outline of a rocky island within the white mist. I step off
the ladder onto a firm surface and find myself on a dirt
trail that winds its way to a spiral mountain trail. This
walkway is like a strand of DNA, and as I climb, I feel
myself changing as if taller, stronger, wiser, and calmer
somehow. I feel like a goddess or queen.*

*When I get to the top I see a man on a high plateau, not
a man actually, but a boy with beautiful dark eyes and
hair, dressed in Indian attire. He has a white turban on
his head and looks very regal. He holds my hands and I
feel love and light fill my heart. I ask for guidance and
he fills my heart with courage. I know I will always
have him as one of my guides. His calm, androgynous
voice is familiar and he tells me I will hear his guidance
through my intuition any time I need it.*

Upper Realms

In chapter 3 you may have practiced journeying to upper
levels from your Great Tree or mystical ladder, or with
the help of various spirit animals and allies. Basically,
the Upper Worlds are just that: they are above your
place of power in the Middle World and are in vary-
ing levels, from the one I call Mt. Olympus to a level
of heaven. In this chapter we will visit a few of these
higher realms, but you may find more as you do inde-
pendent journeys using your own intention. Thus far,
I have found a first level that appears like an island in

the clouds; I have journeyed to a high mountain with a goddess at its center; to a crystal palace full of angels; to a Russian temple with invisible spirit allies; and to many more places in the Upper World.

Where I go most frequently now is to a level of heaven where my husband meets me. Directly in front of me when I land is a path leading to a Greek temple built of white marble with columns and white steps. Up to the left is where some members of my soul family stand, such as my parents. In the middle are more family members from all my incarnations, such as Socrates, a Druid priestess named Brittany, Laloa, a Samoan warrior, and others. To the right and up some steps are the four angels that helped me incarnate this lifetime. Further to the right are the Sacred Library and a garden where I meet with my divine teachers. Your own Upper World will be different from mine, and will be exactly what is perfect for you. More is said about this level of heaven in the pages that follow and in the following chapter.

Portals to the Upper Worlds

The sun is a very powerful portal. It's important that we learn how to travel through the sun's energy because we must pass through it to get to a level of heaven where our soul family, divine teachers, and loved ones can be found.

At times when traveling to the Upper Worlds, you may find other penetrable barriers besides the sun. There can be dense mist and clouds, thick spray as if from a large waterfall, or other energy-like membranes to pass through. In fact, these boundaries offer a sign that we are traveling beyond the Middle World and are now in the Upper World.

> *I find myself flying to the Upper World with Snake and Lao Tzu, and I can't see the way ahead, the is air so full of mist and clouds. We just hold on to each other and finally land on something more solid, but still the mist keeps us from seeing very far. We are climbing upward, and as we do so the mist begins to lift. I see we are on a hedged path, which turns into a labyrinth, and I walk alone to its center. The hedges fall away and jewels like enormous pearls line the edges of the spiral.*

> *I want to see my parents, and set this intention as I fly skyward on Phoenix, my white spirit horse. We soar past the moon and stars and into a realm of high mountains, waterfalls, and rolling mist. Landing on a rock ledge with the falls to the right, I see something moving on the other side of the mist. My parents step out so I can see them, then retreat beyond the spray. I can't seem to touch them here, but can hear them say, "We love you and are so proud of you." With tears streaming down my face, I manage to say, "Thank you for birthing and loving me, for giving me the freedom to make mistakes, and the freedom to find my own path."*

Although this journey gave me some comfort, I have been able to see my parents and spend time with them more intimately in a level of heaven that exists beyond the sun. For this reason and others I now travel primarily through the sun, but it is good to begin by traveling through an easier force field, such as the clouds leading to Mt. Olympus.

Mt. Olympus

I call this first Upper World "Mt. Olympus," because of how it looks: a floating island in the sky with clouds all around it and god-like beings in attendance. If you have studied Greek mythology, you know that the gods and goddesses live on Mt. Olympus, a world where they are immortal and feast on ambrosia. The gods and goddesses also interact with humans and give certain heroes and favored ones their protection and support.

In this case, you are the heroes and heroines, and the elevated beings you meet here truly want to assist you. In your first journey to a place that looks like Mt. Olympus, you will encounter beings such as gods, goddesses, avatars, gurus, ascended masters, historical figures, ancestors, and, in general, highly evolved teachers that will share their wisdom for your transformation.

Check-In

What do you know of Greek or world mythology?

Are there gods, goddesses, heroes, or heroines from mythology that you are drawn to?

Using your own imagination, how do you envision the upper worlds, including heaven?

Sacred Guides and Teachers

Warm wind carries me up to a desert world of rock and mountains. Suddenly, a great rumbling breaks the mountain in two, and in the dust, a white city is there in spiraling levels up into the cosmos. I begin walking through two levels, and follow my intuition outside the city and into a cave. Inside the cave is a Middle Eastern young man with beautiful brown eyes full of kindness. I ask him his name and he says it is Rama. He tells me that he is the incarnation of Krishna and has been with me in all my lives. He calls me "pupil" and says he is my sacred guide.

Rama is my main guide. In doing research, I found that he is indeed the incarnation of Krishna in Hinduism. As a reminder, your guide is a being who has been with you through all your incarnations. This highly evolved spiritual being is the wisdom keeper, and can assist you with everything concerning your life and destiny. In this chapter you have an opportunity to meet a wisdom keeper who may be a guide or teacher assigned to you. Usually these spirit beings appear in human form and will converse with you. At times, however, they appear as light or like a hologram, and at other times they are invisible.

When meeting your teacher or guide on Mt. Olympus, don't be surprised if all you hear is a voice:

> *I fly on wings to the Upper World, this time to a white marble palace. Walking down long corridors, I find myself entering a topaz-colored room, and it is like being inside an enormous jewel. I stand there for some time and feel confused, for there is no one there. Then, just when I think nothing is happening, a melodic voice says, "Welcome. I am the invisible one. You will only hear me. Please sit in the velvet chair and ask your question."*

• •

Check-In

What questions might you ask your teacher or guide?

• •

Intention and Protection

The intention for this journey to the first Upper World, Mt. Olympus, is simply to spirit travel to your personal place of power in the Middle World, look for a way up, and then travel to the Upper World. Also, set the intention to meet with a teacher or guide in this higher realm and to ask questions about your life.

You can ask for protection in whatever way works for you, perhaps saying something like, "I ask for assistance to travel safely to and from Mt. Olympus, to meet with a guide or teacher."

Journey to Mt. Olympus

Prepare as you have for many previous journeys, begin the drumming and go into trance. Now in a relaxed state, follow your intention to your personal place in nature. When you arrive, look for a way up. Once at the top, intend to have something come to carry you to the Upper World.

As you begin to move upward, look for a place in the sky that appears. It might look like an island or a disk in the clouds, but it looks more solid than the air through which you've been traveling. Intend to land on this world and to follow your intuition to a teacher or guide waiting for you.

Spend time with this sacred being, asking questions or listening to your guide or teacher. When the drum speeds up, say good-bye and thank you and find your way back to the Middle World. Walk out to where you began, and then, taking a deep breath, open your eyes.

Check-In

How did you travel to the Upper World?

Describe "Mt. Olympus" or this first Upper World.

Did you meet a teacher or guide? What is the teacher's name? Describe this person.

What did your teacher or guide tell you?

If you choose to do research, record your findings in your journal.

From now on you can journey to meet your spirit teacher or guide in this Upper World any time you need guidance, healing, and the reminder that you are loved and not alone.

Mythical Realms

I sit on the bench in my place of power, holding Lao Tzu's hand and with Snake around my shoulders. I tell them I want to go to Avalon, the sacred isle of the Druids, written about in the King Arthur legends. I climb on Snake's back and we fly steadily until an island appears in the mist.

After landing, I walk toward a grove of trees and suddenly feel people around me. I see their footprints, yet they are the invisible spirits of Avalon, leading me to the sacred grove where Vivienne and the priestesses are engaged in ceremony.

I ask Vivienne how I can become the equivalent of a priestess in this modern age. She says, "You are already a teacher, a minister, a singer, a poet, and a counselor, all duties of the ancient Druids. You do need to spend more time in nature, absorbing the energy of the sun, moon, and stars." Vivienne leads me to the sacred pool and I enter its milky liquid to be cleansed and purified for my return to my world and my purpose.

Avalon is the mythical world that draws me the most, perhaps because I had a past life as a Druid priestess, am of Celtic ancestry, have lived in the UK, and have read many books about the Celts and the Druids. Whenever I need healing and renewal I journey to Avalon and soak in its magic pool. I have also traveled to other mythical realms in the Upper World, such as castles, palaces, temples, and crystal caves.

Perhaps you have read stories of such mythical places, seen films about them, or had dreams about such magical kingdoms. If so, you may have a place in mind. One of my clients has always loved the book *Lost Horizon*, which she read when she was twelve. In a recent journey, she found herself traveling up to a world that looked just like Shangri-La, complete with mystical mountains, green valleys, and abundant rivers, pools, trees, and flowers; in other words, she found a paradise, and more importantly, *her* paradise. In the following journeys, you will have a chance to travel to your own mythical kingdom.

Famous Mythical Places

In my journey described above, I traveled to Avalon, where some say King Arthur is buried. If you have an affinity with King Arthur as I do, or with the Druids and Celts, this might be a place you wish to visit. If this isn't your interest, perhaps you remember stories of Shangri-La, Asgard, Atlantis, Camelot, El Dorado, the Garden of Eden, Lemuria, or Valhalla. Most of us have, at some point, been enchanted by stories of a hidden or elusive paradise. I wanted to be an archeologist in college just because it sounded so romantic to unearth civilizations and find buried treasure and lost cities.

You may also be drawn to the places in fairy tales, such as the castles in *Cinderella* or *Snow White*, or perhaps the elf kingdom of Rivendell in Tolkien's *The Lord of the Rings* trilogy. If you have ever read *The Chronicles of Narnia* by C. S. Lewis, you may still feel enchanted by a portal to the magical world of Narnia with its waterways, giant trees, and talking animals. One of my favorite mythical places is the Land of Oz, with its fields of poppies and magical city and castle. Just use your imagination and think about a place that captivates you. Speaking of Oz, here is what happened in one of my journeys:

> *I climb my Tree of Life and a cyclone comes and whirls me up higher and higher in a spinning vortex of energy. Soon we slow down and I find myself in another world, resembling a park with green grass and picnic tables. I hear my name and walk to a nearby table, and am surprised to find Dorothy, the Tin Man, the Lion, the Scarecrow, and the Wizard all sitting*

around, as if waiting for me. They tell me I am walking my own yellow brick road and meeting my own soul family right on earth. Each of them offers a bit of wisdom: "Follow your heart; use your mind wisely; have courage, keep walking, and never give up." Then a bright red, yellow, and blue hot air balloon comes and takes me higher on new adventures.

Here is another journey that resembles a fairy tale:

After journeying through dense mist and climbing through a trap door in the clouds, I find myself riding a white stallion through a forest toward a shining castle in the distance with a spiral road leading to its gates. Once at the castle, I walk up stairs to the turret, where an old woman with grey hair is waiting. She tells me she is the Goddess of Desire, and she asks what I want in my heart. I say, "Abundance in every way: a great relationship with my husband and family, travel, satisfying work, creative projects in painting and writing, new books to publish, plenty of money, and great joy in all I do." Each time I mention what I want, it becomes a tangible object and a great bird takes it and flies away, leaving a shower of gold dust as it leaves. Then she takes a magic wand and sprinkles me with the same gold from head to foot, twirling me around and laughing.

This Upper World journey took me inside a fairy tale, much like *Cinderella*, yet with a storyline to match what I needed at the time. Just follow your intuition about mythical places, and see which ones seem most appealing.

One intriguing mythical kingdom is Shangri-La, the beautiful valley described in James Hilton's 1933 novel *Lost Horizon*. He did research on Tibetan Buddhist tradition concerning the idea of Shambhala, a pure, heavenly place where the worthy go. The author found that Tibetan Buddhists speak of a mystical kingdom hidden in the Himalaya Mountains. Calling it Shangri-La, Hilton places his version in the western end of the Kunlun Mountains. If you do research on Shangri-La, you will find that the Nazis and others sent expeditions to Tibet, China, and northern Pakistan, looking for this lost paradise. They never found it, but the idea still entices travelers to this day.[30]

Atlantis and Lemuria are both mythical lost continents, the first supposedly at the bottom of the Atlantic Ocean and the second in the Indian or Pacific Ocean. Stories abound concerning these kingdoms, where an advanced race once lived. I have journeyed to Atlantis and believe I had a past life there. What I found were narrow streets and whitewashed buildings, with colorful murals on the walls and people working on metaphysical projects such as telepathy, clairvoyance, astral projection, and telekinesis. I've visited this world twice, and each time I have learned more about the people and their projects. Some researchers say that Atlantis sank due to the misuse of magic and spiritual power.[31]

Asgard and Valhalla come from Norse mythology, Asgard being the heavenly city of the gods ruled by

Odin. Valhalla means "hall of the slain" and is a majestic hall in Asgard where the souls of heroes go after death. Odin chooses half the soldiers to go to Valhalla, and the other half of the slain go to the realm of the goddess Freyja. The movie *Thor* gave viewers a glimpse of these Norse realms. If this mythology appeals to you, you can do further research.

El Dorado (meaning "the golden one") is the mythical lost city of gold in South America that so many have tried to find, especially Spanish explorers such as Francisco Pizarro. Originally, the story began with the ritual of a king covering his body with gold dust and then diving into a lake in Colombia. Since then, the myth expanded to include a lost city of gold supposedly near Lake Parime in the highlands of Guyana in South America.[32] No city of gold has ever been found, but the idea has captured the imagination of rulers and explorers for generations.

The Garden of Eden is well known as the paradise described in the book of Genesis in the Bible. It is a perfect place, where food is abundant on the trees, and pure water flows freely. Writers have used the idea of the Garden when speaking of original innocence and grace before the "fall" of humans when they disobeyed God. You could journey to the Garden in its perfect state as a place of beauty, abundance, and peace.

There are many more mythical places, and you can find them by doing more research. Whether you want to choose a place first, as I did with Avalon, or just ask to travel to a mythical kingdom that would be most illuminating for you, this journey proves to be an adventure.

Intention and Protection

Your intention is to travel to a mythical realm, explore it, and return with a description and knowledge. If you encounter any spirit beings there, you can engage with them. You may want to take a gift (energetically) and receive one when you leave.

For protection, just say whatever works for you, such as, "Please take me to a mythical kingdom (state which one if you wish), and back again, safely."

Journey to a Mythical Place

Get ready to journey as you have in the past, listening to the drum, and begin to find your way to your place of power. Once there, climb to the top of your tree or other high place. Set your intention to travel to a mythical world, and say which one if you have decided. Find yourself traveling to this world, on or with a helper, noticing what levels you pass on your way.

Once you arrive, use all your senses to explore where you are. Take your time to navigate this kingdom, and enjoy exploring. Notice anything that you find especially important to record later. If you want to meet someone, just intend to do so. Then connect with one or more spirit beings and engage them in conversation. Ask whatever you wish to know, or just ask them for guidance.

When the drum speeds up, say good-bye and thank you, and make your way back to your place in nature, walk to your starting point, take several breaths, stretch, then come all the way back and open your eyes.

Check-In

What "transportation" did you use to travel to a mythical place?

What mythical kingdom did you visit on this journey? Describe it.

Did you meet a spirit being there? If so, describe this being.

What did you talk about, or what wisdom did you receive?

More Mythical Journeys

You can choose to travel to another mythical realm in the Upper World, and actually to as many spirit kingdoms as you want. It's up to you. If you wish to do another journey now, you can, or wait and choose another place to visit later. Just know that you can use the same directions, intention, protection statement, and follow-up questions as used in the above journey. Any time you wish to explore a new mythical Upper World, you know the way.

Levels of Heaven

I climb to the top of my tree and Swan is waiting. On the way to heaven we pass the moon, stars, and a Russian palace I have visited before. We soar through the energy of the sun and land in my version of heaven. For a moment I stand and look at this level of heaven with its white beach, marble stepping stones, and stairs leading up to a Greek temple, complete with columns and a long porch. To the left is where my parents usually stand on the top steps, and to the right is where I first met my angels years ago. In the middle, just in front of the temple, are members of my soul family, most of whom I do not recognize.

While still standing in front of the path, I look up higher above the temple and see something I've never seen before: a golden city with facets of crystal reflecting the light, prisms glinting and blinding in their brilliance. Then above this city are spirals of golden light rising into infinity. I sense that I have been given a glimpse of a higher level of heaven, but feel I cannot go there because I am still embodied.

In all honesty, I never truly believed there was a golden city in heaven as the Bible expresses in Revelation 21:18: ". . . the city was pure gold, clear as glass," and yet, I experienced this city directly and exactly as it is described. In a journey a month ago I saw another city below the golden one, a silver and deep blue city on the same plane as my level of heaven with soul family and teachers. The first time I visited this silver city, it seemed as if no one was there, but I could feel energy and realized the souls were there but were invisible to me. I have now visited this blue and silver city a second time, and while walking through the streets, I did see them as light-filled holograms that drifted and flowed past me. Through direct experience using shamanic journeying, we can prove to ourselves that a heavenly realm exists, and that we can visit it while still alive.

The above journey also helped me understand that there isn't just one level in the Upper World of heaven. Perhaps an infinite number exist, as several religious texts express. I have proven this to myself by visiting the realms presented in this chapter, from Mt. Olympus to upper mystical kingdoms, as well as a level of heaven. In the next two chapters you meet your soul family and divine teachers in a level of heaven, and visit loved ones who are now in spirit. This chapter is an introduction to this mystical and sacred heavenly realm.

Check-In

What are your beliefs concerning heaven, paradise, or "the world on high"?

What do you think your level of heaven will look like? Have you had dreams or visions of heaven?

Who do you hope to find there?

Do you feel any resistance, doubt, superstition, or fear about visiting heaven?

Where Is Heaven?

Recently I attended a memorial and took comfort in a speaker's words about the afterlife. He pointed to a long rope behind him, and held up the end with about two inches of black tape. The rest of the rope trailed behind him at least thirty feet. He said that the end with the tape represents our life here, and the rope, our life in heaven, and implied that the best is yet to come. I could see the family of the deceased relax at his words, thinking of their loved one in his new home.

Since the memorial, I've been thinking about our life here and our afterlife quite a bit. I agree with the minister in that I, too, feel there is no death, and I believe that we are immortal. The only issue I have with believing that the best is yet to come, and that this life is only a preparation for the next, is that we may not live as fully here, may not live in the present moment and savor its beauty and connect with those we love as closely.

What if we live here with the intention of being the best people we can be: loving, generous, kind, compassionate, unselfish, thoughtful, honest, loyal, full of purpose and in service, not because our reward is in heaven, but because we want to live lives that are meaningful and of worth?

What if we live our soul's purpose, staying present within ourselves and with others, and we do this so we raise our consciousness and our vibration, evolving each moment into the highest humans we can be? This means we are also happy here, living our dreams with passion, loving others deeply, and helping them live lives that are meaningful, too.

Then aren't we creating and living in heaven on earth? I believe we can live a heavenly life here, and that once we are spirits, we can continue to evolve higher and higher in heaven. In this way, our lives as spiritual beings are seamless; we can transform here while still embodied, and continue to evolve as souls free of our physical form. I am looking forward to no longer having a body and just being a spirit, but I am going to savor life as a human while I can. I want to feel sun on my face and swim in the sea, eat my favorite foods and dance the night away; I want to wrap my arms around my children and friends and tell them I love them. Why not love where we are and look forward to where we're going?

So, to answer the question, "Where is heaven?" I have to say it is both where we go after death, and what we can create while alive. Here in this chapter we are mainly referring to the place we go in the afterlife, but in chapter 8 we will be discussing how to create heaven here.

Views of Heaven and the Afterlife

Every major religion describes the place souls go after death, some more directly and some more subtly, and the places vary from an underworld to a kingdom on high. In Greek and Roman literature, heaven and hell exist in an underworld, and souls are assigned one place or the other. Those who are punished go to Tartarus, and those pure souls go to the Elysian Fields. The only deviation from this view that I've found comes from the Roman Cicero, who describes souls traveling high above the earth after death and looking down on a small planet far away.[33]

The Egyptians believed that they would experience rebirth after death if they were respectful of the gods, were mummified, and had statues of themselves placed in the tombs. They believed that one's soul went to the Fields of Aaru, but the body and personality went to the Kingdom of the Dead.[34] It is interesting that the Egyptians and some Christian faiths have one similar belief: death is not the end, just a temporary event, and eternal life could be ensured for devoted souls.

The Hindu book *Bhagavad Gita* speaks of the soul discarding the old body and taking on a new one, the body being a shell and the soul inside, immutable and infinite, taking on a different life in the cycle of birth and death. If one's cycle of reincarnation ends, it is called Mukti, which means staying with God forever. Hindus believe that when someone dies, the god of death, Yama, sends helpers to get the soul from the person's body. Then the soul travels down a dark tunnel toward the south. The soul reincarnates itself based on the deeds in the previous life. Bad karma would mean returning as an animal or lower creature, and good karma would guarantee having a happy life in a good family.[35]

When Buddha came he helped followers to end the cycle of reincarnation. *The Tibetan Book of the Dead* explains that the dead person will see a bright light that shows a path to move upward and leave the pattern of death and rebirth. It is believed that wandering souls receive help from different Buddhas who lead them to the light and the path to an immortal realm. Sometimes souls are fearful and do not follow the path or the light, and then they must reincarnate.[36]

In the Jewish Talmud the afterlife is also described. First, the soul is brought for judgment, and those pure souls enter Olam Haba, or the "World to Come." Most souls must first undergo a review of their lives and what they have done wrong. Then these souls must undergo a spiritual purification before moving on. The medieval Spanish and Jewish philosopher Maimonides says that an afterlife continues for every human being when the soul is released from the "house" of the body.[37]

It is in Christianity that the word "heaven" is primarily used. Heaven is referred to in both the old and new testaments of the Bible, and Christian sects differ in their views of heaven and an afterlife. Most Christian faiths teach that there is a heaven and a hell, and that those who have done good deeds or are chosen by God go to heaven. Those who have sinned, have denied God, or have not been saved by Jesus, go to hell. Latter Day Saints or Mormons believe that the soul existed before birth and will exist after death. They also believe that the soul keeps progressing through levels after death.[38] Some Christian faiths also believe in Purgatory, and a discussion of this in-between level appears in chapter 7.

Universalists believe that salvation is for everyone, but Seventh-day Adventists teach that sinners are destroyed. The Gospel of John states that only if people accept Jesus will they be given eternal life, and Jesus also says that a time would come when the tombs would be opened and the dead would hear his voice; those who had led good lives would be granted resurrection, and those who had been evil would be condemned.

In the Catholic faith it is taught that levels exist in the afterlife: heaven, purgatory, and hell. Catholics teach that the soul is separated from the body at the moment of death, that the soul is immortal and never ceases to exist. The soul is judged and then is sent to heaven if the person is pure, to hell if the individual has sinned, and to purgatory if the soul can be purged of any minor sins before going to heaven. Moderate Catholics are currently rejecting the idea of purgatory and hell to some degree, and believing more strongly in heaven for all.[39]

Bahá'í writings state that the soul is immortal and will continue to progress after death until attaining God's presence. People of the Bahá'í faith believe that souls retain their individuality and consciousness and can recognize and communicate with other souls they have known, such as spouses, other family members, and friends. The Bahá'í writings express that souls in the afterlife have different levels of growth and consciousness, are aware of their past actions, and understand the consequences. Those who have lived a life focused on God will feel great joy in the heavenly world, and those who have made mistakes will be aware of what they have done and will want to make up for their errors. Souls can recognize and connect with those at the same spiritual level.[40]

Check-In

What are your beliefs about the afterlife and heaven?

After reading about the afterlife and heaven above, are there beliefs that appeal to you?

Research and Practice

You may be intrigued by some of the religious and spiritual beliefs listed above. Perhaps do research on one or more of them. Also, you may wish to visit one of the churches, temples, synagogues, or other houses of worship mentioned earlier. If you already follow a faith or have a spiritual practice, then it might be a good time to go to a service, do some reading, do a ritual, say prayers, or, in other ways, fill with spiritual food that agrees with you and satisfies.

Record any research or share your spiritual practices in your journal.

Intention and Protection

In the following journey, your intention is to spirit travel to your personal place of power. Find a way up, then intend that a being carry you or travel with you through the sun to a level of heaven. Ask for a spirit being to come that is protective. This is an introductory journey meant to familiarize you with a heavenly realm.

A protection phrase can be whatever you like to say. You may want to light a candle to honor your sacred journey.

Journey to a Level of Heaven

This spirit journey is similar to others in this chapter except this one definitely takes the sun route. Some shamans suggest that you ask for more protection for this journey and travel with a being that loves and protects you. This could be an animal helper such as a bird or other creature, or it could be an angelic being, a pod of light, or other means of travel that feels right to you.

Once you have said your statement of protection and you know your intention, get yourself ready to journey in the way that works for you. Start your recording and begin to journey first to your place of power.

Once in the highest place in your natural world, ask for an ally to come. Get in, on, or fly next to this being, and soar upward past the moon and stars, past mythical realms you may have visited, and then through the sun's energy. Set the silent intention to travel through the sun easily and out the other side.

After you have exited, begin looking for the level of heaven where you will land. It might appear as an island in the sky, or it may be a bigger landmass. Just allow whatever is meant to appear to do so naturally and effortlessly.

When you have landed, remember that the object of this journey is to explore this level of heaven. You will take other journeys in the next few chapters to meet your soul family and divine teachers, as well as loved ones. All you need to do in this journey is use your senses to explore this new world. If beings come to you, you can engage with them, but know that your main purpose is just to find and visit this Upper World.

Once the drum speeds up, look around and breathe in the intention that you will remember this place and come again. Find your means of travel and come back through the sun, and back to your place of power. Return to your starting point, and with a few deep breaths, open your eyes.

• •

Check-In

What helped transport you to a level of heaven?

What was it like to travel through the sun?

Describe your level of heaven.

Did you see or talk to anyone there? Describe any encounters.

Overall, how did it feel to visit your level of heaven?

• •

An Open Door

Now that you have traveled to several Upper Worlds, an important door has opened for you, a door leading to more encounters with those in the spirit world. You know your way to the higher realms now, and you can find your way back. In the chapters that follow, you will be returning to a level of heaven to meet your soul family, your divine teachers, and departed loved ones. This is an exciting time because you are about to embark on a journey that most people only experience during death or after transition.

But, as you probably realize from previous journeys, you don't have to die to go to heaven! You are soaring to upper realms now, meeting teachers, guides, mythical beings, avatars, gods, goddesses, heroes, and others. In this chapter you have experienced a level of heaven and now can visit beings that love you in this sacred realm, asking for their wisdom in order to transform yourself and your life while still alive. What a blessing to know that you are not alone, that you are loved beyond measure, and that you are immortal.

➣ 6 ➢

A Level of Heaven

Let me be light.

Not jagged lightning
scarring redwoods
nor wildfire burning
the bears' home. Not
a meteor striking
the earth, nor sun
melting icecaps.

No, let me be the firefly
reflecting moonbeams,
a glowing star lighting
a path to heaven. Let me be
the energy of a thousand
Tinker Bells shining my light
everywhere, for everyone.

Let me be the light of love.

—From my poem "Let Me Be Light"

I am a tiger running to the edge of the earth and jumping into the sun. As I fly I become myself, soaring through and beyond the sun to the Upper World of my soul family. I cry seeing everyone there, my parents, my Aunt Ruth, the man in the white turban, Socrates, and all the angels. In front of me is the white Greek temple with marble steps, and to the right, the Library, and beyond the temple grounds, the garden where my divine teachers gather in Sacred School. Suddenly, the domed top of the temple opens, golden light pours down from above, and I feel my spirit rising up beyond the temple. I know I am being filled with the light of the Source, and now I am only light. I hear music all around me, like Rachmaninoff, Beethoven, Vivaldi, and Bach, all mixing and rising in a crescendo, as colors swirl like the aurora borealis. I, too, begin swirling and turning to music and color throughout time and space. I dance in brilliant spirals of light, and am joined by the spirits of my earthly and heavenly families, and then by everyone in all the worlds. We stand in a circle on the earth as it might be seen from outer space, joining hands and singing together. We are one people of one world chanting four words over and over: "We are only love."

I weep even now as I read this aloud. To experience such oneness, such love, and to become universal light is hard to speak about. The miracle of the above experience is that it changed me; it took me to another level in my spiritual growth and in my commitment to being the highest and most evolved I can be in this lifetime. I feel humbled by such a journey, yet know that this honor must be acknowledged through right actions, must be honored by how I live my life.

This chapter can be your own turning point, your own recognition of your gifts and purpose and your own conscious evolution into your highest self. In the next pages you will journey to your own level of heaven, meet your soul family, find and experience at least one past life, receive wisdom from your divine teachers, and, while there, review your contract for this lifetime. As a bonus, you'll go on a journey to meet an esteemed ancestor, ask for a healing, and become light in the process of transfiguration. This chapter encourages you to soar higher, feel more deeply, and realize more meaning than before. The sky is not even the limit for you!

. . . .

Check-In

Have you ever connected with people in real life who feel like soul family, those you deeply connect with on an energy or heart level?

Do you believe in past lives and reincarnation?

Do you have a sense that you have a contract to fulfill this lifetime?

Have you had any spiritual teachers here on earth?

Do you know about any of your ancestors or your family history?

Are you in need of any physical, emotional, or spiritual healing?

What comes up when imagining becoming light?

••

The Soul and Over-Soul

If you believe that you have a soul or spirit and that this soul is immortal and survives the death of your body, then you have good company with some of the world's greatest thinkers, such as Socrates, Plato, Aristotle, Emerson, Thoreau, and many others. I believe in the existence of an individual over-soul, or higher self, and that we are all part of a Universal Over-Soul.

Socrates and Plato taught that the psyche (soul) was the essence of a person, and that this absolute goodness survived after death. They also taught that the immortal soul of an individual would still be able to think after death, feel deep emotions like anger and love, and feel bodily desire.[41] Perhaps this is why my husband and I can speak to one another, feel deeply, and even make love on an energy level as two souls in a level of heaven.

These ancient philosophers also said that the eternal part of us, our soul, would live on but also be continually reborn in a new body. Socrates often said that the most important thing we must do as humans is to care for our souls by rising above our physical appetites and this physical world. He believed that the body was often an obstacle to attaining true wisdom and goodness within our souls. At death, it was Socrates' hope that he had overcome his body and the physical world and could join the gods in immortality.[42]

I agree with Plato's definition and description of the soul, and his view of the over-soul. Plato describes the over-soul as absolute goodness, something beyond description and knowable only through intuition. Ralph Waldo Emerson uses Greek philosophy in his essay "The Over-Soul," in which he says that the human soul is immortal, vast, and beautiful; that the ego is lesser in comparison but given too much power and credence as our true selves; and that everyone's souls are connected. He implies that we are God or have the essence of God within us. When discussing the over-soul, Emerson uses terms like unity, common heart, wisdom, virtue, power, wholeness, universal beauty to which every part and particle is equally related, and the eternal one.[43]

When I read works by Emerson and Henry David Thoreau, I picture a vast orb of light or a swirling vortex of colors, and this to me represents the Universal Over-Soul, with each of us joined to this orb, perhaps with a cord of light from our individual souls to this collective soul, all of us joined in oneness. In fact, my journey shared earlier illustrates this image of all of creation connected in wholeness as part of a Universal Over-Soul.

I love this concept and image of soul connection, and on a more individual level, I also embrace the concept that each of us has what I call the higher self, or as some shamanic teachers call it, the personal over-soul. We can connect with our higher self or personal over-soul in the Upper World, and once connected we can hear messages and guidance from our higher self through our intuition, which seems to speak to us first in the heart, and then through the mind. We can learn to trust in our higher soul-selves, and connect to the highest vibration in the cosmos that some call God,

Source, Spirit, the Unified Field, the Mind of God, the Universe, the Creative Force, or the Universal Over-Soul. You will have a chance to connect with your own higher self and "The Field" in an exercise that follows.

For those of you who are more scientific, think of God as universal energy, just as quantum field theorists describe the universe as non-material, and atoms as non-solid states of energy and information. I like Deepak Chopra's idea that thoughts are the same impulse of energy and information that form the universe, and he speaks of God in these terms: "And what could be better than to use for our model the mind of God, the unified field, the field of all possibilities." Chopra continues to describe this unified field or God when he writes, "This invisible nothingness silently orchestrates, instructs, guides, governs, and compels nature to express itself with infinite creativity, infinite abundance, and unfaltering exactitude into a myriad of designs and patterns and forms."[44]

The idea of the Unified Field is further explored by Allen Roland, who says that it is a psychic energy field made up of universal love, that time and space do not exist there, and that we can instantly be in the past, present, and future at once; that it is a place of unity and completeness, fulfilling all beings with an evolving, loving plan.[45] Scientists are looking closely at Roland's work, and those of us who have been to this Unified Field through our own direct shamanic experience know that it exists.

Some shamanic teachers like Alberto Villoldo feel that using theories such as the Unified Field and the language of quantum physics can devalue shamanism, which is tens of thousands of years old. I agree, and at the same time, know that I have used quantum physics to explain my work in energy medicine to those needing a scientific explanation. I hope that reading this text and having direct experience of spirit worlds will change the way you speak about the universe, perhaps by including terms such as higher self, personal over-soul, and a collective or Universal Over-Soul.

Many people are tired of Newtonian Materialism, are tired of this construct that hasn't helped them feel more passion and joy or find their purpose. A renewed interest in quantum physics is causing people to pause and discern that everything is energy, including us. This feeling of connection with all things can help us unite as a species and consciously evolve individually and collectively.

The following exercise can help you strengthen your connection to your intuition through your higher self or personal over-soul, and from now on, this can help you transform and more easily chart and navigate your life path.

Meeting Your Higher Self

After flying through the sun, I pass through mist and find myself in a level of heaven in front of a beautiful crystal temple. The doors open and I go inside and sit in a waiting area with wooden benches facing one another. After some time, a door opens and a tall, majestic woman comes out, with long brown hair in waves and a flowing white gown. She looks like me but is taller, straighter, more light-filled, and exuding powerful energy. At times she changes into a hologram

of golden light, and then back into a human figure.
She smiles radiantly and comes toward me, takes my
hands, lifts me up and embraces me warmly, as if we
are dearest friends who have been apart. In a way this
is true; she is the highest part of who I am, my higher
self, and we are finally in connection. We sit and talk
for what seems like hours and she tells me she is the
voice of my intuition and that I will hear her more
clearly from now on. When it is time for me to leave,
I feel her energy in my heart.

The above journey has helped me know with
certainty that I have a higher self that speaks to me
through intuition. When making a decision, I hear a
voice leading me to the right choice. This has become
easier over the years, and now it is an instant knowing
or sensing from my higher self or intuition. I usually
feel it as a sensation in my body and heart first, and
then the words come in my mind. More and more often
I also see images of what I am to do next, whether it
is a road to take, a person to contact, a food to eat, or
anything I am deciding. My higher self, not my ego, is
in charge most of the time, and I can tell the difference
in their voices and messages.

You, too, can meet your higher self or personal
over-soul, who is the wisest part of you, the one vibrating at the highest frequency, as the most conscious
and evolved aspect of who you are. In the following
journey, your higher self may look like you or perhaps
be like a hologram or light being, or it may appear as
colors, sound, or energy waves. If your higher self does
not appear, you may sense a presence and hear a voice
speak in your mind.

Once you meet your higher self, your life can change profoundly. No longer will you just have the ego voice making decisions, and not always with your greatest good at heart, but you will have a higher part of yourself helping you create more balance and harmony.

Intention and Protection

The intention for this journey is to travel to the Upper World and to a level of heaven to meet with your higher self. For protection, you can say whatever works for you, or something like, "Please help me travel safely to and from a meeting with my higher self in a level of heaven. Thank you."

Higher Self Journey

Start the drumming recording and begin imagining yourself on the path to your sacred power place. Once in your natural world, look for a place to climb up, and at the top intend for a helper to arrive to take you to a level of heaven. Travel through the sun and then arrive in a level of heaven. Follow your intuition to the place where you will meet your higher self. Use all your senses to take in this place, and once your higher self arrives, notice everything about this being.

Now meet with your higher self and converse, with the words coming in your mind. No matter their appearance or essence, whether in human form or in a more amorphous state, you can communicate with them. You may ask questions or just ask for wisdom about your life. Take in everything you can and feel the higher frequency of this being; breathe in this energy and feel the connection between you. If you wish, hug or hold your higher self and feel a merging of your energy filling your heart.

Once the drumming speeds up, it is time to thank your higher self and say good-bye. Find your way back to your helper, fly to your Middle World, climb down onto your path and back to the starting point. Take several deep breaths, stretch, and move your body. When ready, open your eyes.

· ·

Check-In

Describe your higher self.

What did you talk about, or what wisdom did you receive?

Did you feel the energy of your higher self? How?

· ·

Higher Self Meditation

It is time to invite the energy of your higher self into your heart space so that you will be able to access greater wisdom through your intuition anytime you wish. From now on, the energy and voice of your higher self will be available within you.

You can use the drumming recording or just use your breath to do this guided visualization. Take several deep breaths, and with eyes closed, take your deepest breath yet, and on the exhale, imagine yourself journeying into the world of your own body, into the realm of your heart space.

You are magical in this state and can easily travel down, down, all the way down and into the heart space in your chest. Once there, as you would do in any realm, look around and explore using all your senses. Since this is where your higher self will be, create something beautiful, either a lovely place in nature or even a temple or palace. You want to envision a place of beauty for the highest part of you.

Once you are happy with the place, invite in your higher self, the being you met in a level of heaven. Sometimes he or she will be a brighter version of you; sometimes this being will be more energy than form, and can appear as light or in another way. Just invite your higher self to come now.

Experience the arrival or your higher self and invite this being to spend time with you. Notice everything about them, especially their energy and their voice. You may ask questions or just ask for wisdom and take it all in. Feel the comfort of being with this part of you that wants the highest and best for you at all times. Listen intently, and again hear this being's voice in order to recognize it from now on.

When your experience feels complete or the drumming speeds up, thank your higher self. Perhaps embrace, if it feels right, and know that from now on the voice of your higher self will be within you, heard as your intuition. Say good-bye to your higher self, and taking a deep breath in, feel yourself traveling up, up out of your heart space, and on the exhale, breathe yourself back into your whole body. Take a few more breaths, stretch, and on a final breath, come all the way back to the room and open your eyes.

Check-In

Write about your experience of welcoming your higher self into your heart.

Now that you have connected more deeply with your higher self or personal over-soul, perhaps you can feel your own soul essence more strongly. Knowing that you are a soul within a body will help you connect with your own soul family in a level of heaven.

Soul Family

I fly on Eagle's back to the Upper World and expect to see my husband Tom waiting for me, but my parents are there with our Irish setter, Rusty, who is running on the sand. My mother puts her arm through mine and we walk a new way, to the left and up the beach. We sit on a bench under a shady gazebo and talk. She tells me I now need to be my own mother in the way I treat myself, by following my intuition each moment. She tells me to ask myself, "What do I need right now?" and an answer will come. As we stand up, a rocking chair appears and I sit on my mother's lap with a blue blanket over me, and she sings and rocks me. As I relax more and more, I feel the presence of others and look up to see Jesus and an African man in tribal attire standing over me, hands outstretched, and I know they are healing me.

~

Swan carries me to the Upper World, and I see a crowd there to greet us. My mother is the first to embrace me, and whispers, "You are never alone. We love you and are here for you all the time." Arianrhod steps out and tells me to look at the moon and I will feel her and a renewed strength. St. Francis says to be in nature more, to feel bird wings within my heart, opening. Then, Socrates says, "I am also in your soul family and see that you are a teacher as I am. Always be a teacher in the world as you have much to share." Jesus comes to take my hands and says, "I understand how you feel. I, too, have been hurt and heartbroken. Go into the wilderness alone as I did, and get in touch with your heart and your purpose."

My mother, who died several years ago, is not just my guardian angel and loved one in a level of heaven, but she is in my soul family. Our parents and relatives are not always a part of our soul family, but both my parents are, as well as my Aunt Ruth. This means that the three of them have been with me in all my lifetimes, perhaps not always as parents and an aunt, but in some capacity.

Socrates is in my soul family and more and more he is sharing his wisdom with me. The other beings that appeared, such as Arianrhod, St. Francis, and Jesus are guides and teachers that appear in both the Middle and Upper Worlds. My parents and Socrates are the only members of my soul family that have spoken with me, but there are others outside and within the temple.

Your level of heaven will appear just the way you need it, and as you and your soul family have decided it should appear. I was told that my soul family and I agreed that our realm should be in a Greek setting with a white marble temple and library. Your soul family and divine teachers will also be different from mine, and absolutely your own. They have been with you forever and have much to share with you. It will be quite a reunion.

Definitions

What is a soul family? Who are these beings in your level of heaven? From my own direct experience over many years, I believe it is a group of beings in community, linked by their soul lineage over many incarnations. Your own soul family has been with you perhaps from the time your soul came into being. You have the opportunity in this chapter to journey to a level of heaven and meet with members of your soul family.

• •

Check-In

Is there anything you are feeling before this journey to your soul family?

Do you have any expectations you need to release so you can let the experience unfold naturally?

• •

Practice

Think about or spend time with those you consider in your earthly soul family, those you feel connected to on an energy level, heart to heart. Close your eyes and think of them now. After thinking of them or seeing them, write about this connection.

Intention and Protection

Your intention for this journey is to travel to your level of heaven and meet your soul family. You will first go to your place of power, then journey through the sun to the upper realm where you will meet your family. For protection you can say what works for you, or speak this request, "Please help me journey safely through the sun to a level of heaven where I may meet my soul family. Thank you."

Soul Family Journey

Prepare as you have previously, start the recording and let the drum take you more deeply into trance where you find the path to your Middle World.

Once in your high place, intend that a helper appear and take you to your level of heaven. For journeys to this exalted realm, you might want to request a guide or teacher with highly evolved energy. This doesn't have to be a human guide or teacher, but can be an animal teacher that takes you to upper worlds as my Eagle and Swan do.

Travel together to the Upper World, through the membrane of the sun's energy and out again, and to a level of heaven. See this place come into view and land there. Using all your senses, look around and take in everything about this level of heaven. After landing, invite your soul family to appear. Pay attention to their appearance, whether they are in human form or beings of energy and light.

Now interact with your soul family, ask their names, receive wisdom, and remember that their words will come in your mind. When the drum speeds up, say good-bye and thank them, make your way back to your helper, and travel back to your world of personal power. Climb down from your high place and walk your path back to the world of ordinary reality. Take a few deep breaths, move your body, and open your eyes.

· ·

Check-In

Who went with you to a level of heaven?

Describe your level of heaven.

Did you meet your soul family? Describe this encounter.

If you mainly connected with one person, what was shared?

What overall messages did you sense or receive?

· ·

The Library and Past Lives

My Guide Rama and I arrive in my level of heaven where we will visit the Library of Akashic Records, and find my past lives. The library glows with an amber light, and we notice that gold liquid is flowing beneath the bridge and around the building. The library is transparent or translucent like crystal, and reflects the light.

Once inside we walk on what feels like warm clouds, and sit at a crystal table on pillows of cloud. I ask for my Book of Life and it floats down and into my hands. On the bronze and wooden cover is a Tree of Life and the bark and leaves are real; a full moon peers through the branches and an owl is looking at me. The name on the cover is blurry, but it looks like Danus or Danis. I want to experience one of my past lives, and with this thought I am drawn into a hole in the tree.

I find myself in a magical forest with light pouring down. As I think of visiting a past life, the light seems to draw me up, until Rama and I are on the constellation of the Pleiades. Suddenly we are flying through space, and I know we are on a mission to raise the frequency of love in the universe. I'm not at all surprised that this is my purpose in this past life, and feel at home as a light being.

After seeing this past life, I ask to see others and am propelled back to three other lives. I end up in Chako Canyon as a medicine woman, then as a Druid priestess in England, and finally I am in Atlantis working on telepathic communication.

What I am told by an unseen guide in the library is that I am a light worker, a healer-priestess in many lifetimes, and am here to keep bringing the light of knowledge and love to all.

Not all my past lives have been so uplifting, and at times I was submissive and fearful. I was also persecuted for my spiritual beliefs, and in more than one lifetime I lived in a monastery. I have learned from these challenging lives how important it is not to be afraid to stand up for myself, to tell my truth, to be in loving relationships with others, and to live my life authentically. This fascinating path to your past lives, experiencing who you were then, can lead you to a deeper understanding of who you are now, and inspire you to embrace or alter the patterns you find.

Intention and Protection

In this journey you can visit the Library and ask to see your Book of Life. Then you can visit a recent past life or more than one, depending on the time you allot. The purpose is to get a sense of the lives you've led and who you've been in other lifetimes. For protection say whatever you wish, or something like, "Please help me travel safely to and from the Library in a level of heaven, and to my past lives. Thank you." You may want to ask a guide or teacher to travel with you.

Past Life Journey

As the drumming takes you into trance, find yourself on the path to your natural world, and once there, climb to the place that connects you to your upward journeys. Sense that someone or something is coming to take you to a level of heaven; ask for a spirit being that can offer you the most understanding of your experience. When your helper arrives, journey through the sun to your level of heaven. Once you land, follow your intuition to the Library of Akashic Records, and have your guide or teacher go with you.

When inside, ask for your Book of Life, and when you see it, be sure to notice the cover and notice if a name is on it. Also notice a portal or way in that you may find on the cover or inside the book. Be sure to take your guide or teacher with you into the portal and into the past life. Sometimes you will land in a staging area as I did in the forest. If you travel to more than one lifetime, you may want to come back to this staging area and go to other lifetimes from there.

Now journey to one of your more recent lives and learn all you can about who you were and what happened. Just take in as much as you can, sometimes becoming this person, and sometimes as a neutral observer of that lifetime. Notice your dress, the surroundings, and make a guess as to the time period, the location, and what you are doing there. Also, be sure to ask your guide, teacher, or someone at the Library to help you discover any links to this life.

Once the drum speeds up, find your way back through the portal to the Library, and then to where you landed. Fly back through the sun to your power place. Thank your helper and receive any last words of wisdom. Walk your path and come fully back to the world of ordinary reality, taking a breath in and opening your eyes.

Check-In

Who or what ally showed up to accompany you, and how is this significant?

Describe your flight, if it is different from previous ones.

What does your Library look like?

Describe your Book of Life, especially anything on the cover.

Describe this past life, including who you are and what you are doing.

Did you travel to any other lives? If so, describe these lifetimes.

After guidance from a spirit ally and listening to your own intuition, what may be some of your patterns and lessons from previous lives and what are their connections to this life?

Divine Teachers and Sacred School

Rama meets me in my natural world dressed in a beautiful white robe and white turban. He places a red and gold cape around my shoulders and a gold crown on my head. We travel in a spiral pattern to the Upper

World and land near the Library. Right away I hear my favorite music, Pachelbel's Canon in D, wafting from a garden. In this garden we see people standing around talking and laughing and when we enter they applaud and tell us to please join them. We sit in a circle with men and women of various ages and one child.

Suddenly a tablet of light appears above me and floats down. I am told that this is my contract for this life, what I agreed to do for this incarnation. My teachers ask me if it feels accurate, and together we revise the contract to now read,

Light worker:
to bring knowledge
love and healing
to humanity
and planet Earth.

I agree to this contract and they all say I am doing a great job of fulfilling my destiny this lifetime. I am to believe I am limitless, that everything is possible and will be manifested through my right action. Then the group gives me a new cape that is cobalt blue and trimmed with purple velvet and a medallion of a nine-pointed star.

This journey is one of many I have taken to Sacred School in a level of heaven. What I call Sacred School may appear differently for you, and the beings will be those divine teachers assigned to you. These wise ones are here to give you guidance and help you with decisions, especially ones that mean choosing the highest and most noble path.

Unlike some earthly teachers that have been impatient or harsh with us, these divine teachers are compassionate, patient, and loving. They are also very honest and will kindly but firmly suggest that you may be headed in the wrong direction. They will never tell you what to do, but will offer suggestions and guidance, and then you must decide your course of action. Any time you need support, you may want to visit your Sacred School.

Sacred Schools in History

The Sacred School I find in a level of heaven has similarities to the ancient Mystery Schools of India, Egypt, Persia, and Greece. The Mystery Schools are thought to originate in the Near East, especially in India and Egypt. Even Pythagoras, the Greek mathematician and philosopher, traveled to Egypt and was initiated there, but continued through Persia and into India and found very similar and more ancient teachings in these countries.[46]

The most famous Mystery School was in Eleusis near Athens, Greece. In its prime, the school trained students to purify themselves, with the goal to free the soul from the body's dominance. Students went through several stages such as purification, learning traditions and mysteries, introspection, learning how to lead others to knowledge, and communing with God. By his own initiation into the Mystery School, Plato said that he felt liberated from his body and united with his higher self.[47]

Initiation is an ancient practice going back thousands of years, and visiting your Sacred School and divine teachers is, in a sense, initiating you into a new and higher way of being. The purpose of a Mystery School and the shamanic Sacred School is similar: to become more conscious of ourselves as more than bodies, to know we are souls able to transcend the ego, and to listen to and even become our highest selves.

Check-In

Have you ever worked with highly evolved teachers, and if so, what have you learned?

What guidance do you need from your own divine teachers?

Are there any specific questions you wish to ask them?

Intention and Protection

Your intention is to go from your place of power and through the sun to your level of heaven where your divine teachers gather. Spend time with them, ask any questions, and receive their messages. Also, ask to see your contract for this lifetime and revise it if necessary. For protection, you can say whatever works for you.

Journey to Sacred School

Get ready as you usually do, listen to your drumming recording, take a few deep breaths, and begin. Find yourself walking on the path to your Middle World of personal power, climb up to your launching area, greet a guide, teacher, or ally that comes to escort you, and journey to a level of heaven. Once you land, follow your intuition to your own Sacred School and divine teachers and interact with them.

Give and receive information, and let them teach you what you need to learn. Spend time looking around at the beings present and notice if anyone looks familiar; take in the number of people and any details about them that seem important.

At some point, ask to see your contract for this lifetime, review it, and then together decide if it needs revising. By the time you leave this first class in Sacred School, intend that you know what your purpose is for this lifetime based on your contract.

Be sure to thank your teachers for their support. When the drum speeds up, make your way back to the staging area for your return. Once in your Middle World, climb down and walk the path back to ordinary reality. Take a breath or two and open your eyes.

● ●

Check-In

Are there any changes in your place of power or the spirit being that comes?

Once in a level of heaven, where did you find Sacred School? Describe it.

Who are your divine teachers and what did you talk about?

What was your original contract, and if you revised it, what does it say now? Are you already fulfilling this contract, or do you have a new purpose?

. . . .

Evolved Ancestors

Flying to my level of heaven as a white bird, I hear faint music, and then the music becomes distinct: bagpipes. The sound takes me to a familiar place on an ocean shore, and I know this is Scotland. The hills in the distance are bright green and the land is craggy with many rocks. I look up to see several ancestors walking forward to greet me: men with beards, women in long dresses, and children hugging my knees. I look down and see I am dressed in deep blue with a circlet of gold on my head. It is as if I am a royal guest being welcomed home. We walk to a castle and I climb the steps to an upper room and a balcony over the sea. There are dolphins and whales jumping, and I think that this is definitely heaven. A woman comes forward with long auburn hair encircled by an aura of gold light, and I know she is a highly placed ancestor on my father's side, the Allison clan. She tells me that all the ancestors love me deeply and I can call on them any time.

This journey to my ancestors in the Upper World felt so real and familiar. I felt connected to the land and to the people who greeted me. This connection has helped me to feel supported and know that I am never alone. You, too, have ancestors just waiting to meet you. Some may have come to you during your early journeys to your place of power in the Middle World. You can invite them into that world or visit them in the Upper World.

....

Check-In

Do you know of any ancestors from family research, or perhaps from meeting them in your Middle World, that you would like to visit in the Upper World?

How do you feel about being surprised by ancestors you know nothing about?

....

Intention and Protection

The intention for this journey is to travel to the Upper World from your place of power and meet a highly evolved ancestor. You can ask questions or just ask for their guidance. For protection, say whatever works for you.

Ancestor Journey

Prepare for your ancestor journey to the Upper World in ways that have worked before. Use the drum and see yourself on the path to your natural world of power.

Once there, climb up and wait for a guide or teacher to take you to the Upper World. Travel to the upper realms through the sun to the place where you are to meet your exalted ancestor. This may be in your level of heaven or in a world parallel to this higher plane.

When you arrive in an Upper World, look around and notice how this place makes you feel. When you meet your ancestor, notice the person's appearance, and if he or she gives a name and perhaps something about your family lineage. Spend time together asking about your heritage or about anything that intrigues you, and listen to your ancestor share any wisdom.

When the drum speeds up, say good-bye and thank you and travel back to your natural world, walk your path to where you begin and into ordinary reality. Take a few breaths, and, when ready, open your eyes.

Check-In

Where did you go in the Upper World to meet your ancestor? Describe this place.

If an ancestor arrived, describe this person.

What did the two of you talk about?

Did you learn anything about your ancestry or anything to help you now?

If you want to research this ancestor or anything from the journey, write your findings in your journal.

Upper World Healing

I arrive in a level of heaven and my husband Tom is waiting for me. We are both dressed in white robes and Tom tells me we are to meet our teachers, guides, and soul family members for a healing in the temple. Upon entering I see candles, stained glass, and prisms of colored light falling on everyone. We all hold hands and are told to close our eyes and feel the love inside us. I breathe in this infinite love, and all the energy in my body begins to rise up and out my crown chakra. I feel a buzzing in my hands and throughout my body and within my heart, a life force of love. I feel the oneness of all our spirits joining, feel we are one love, one heart, one soul.

I have been blessed to receive many healings in each of the spirit worlds, probably because I need a lot of them! After accidents and injuries or during illnesses, I can journey to one of the worlds, ask for a healing, and it always comes in some form. Several spirit allies, from animal helpers to guides and teachers, have helped me feel better physically, emotionally, and spiritually. The more I ask for help from the unseen realms and from these beautiful spirit beings, the more help comes, even without doing a journey to their worlds. They come to mine.

When my appendix ruptured a few years ago, I was in intense pain and moving in and out of consciousness. Once in the hospital I remember suddenly feeling this warm energy of love and peace inside me, and all around me, removing my pain and holding me in a comforting embrace. My husband told me later that he saw angels all around my bed, and at the time wasn't sure if they were there to heal me or take me with them. All I know is that I felt their energy and that they came to save my life.

Now you can ask for a physical, emotional, or spiritual healing in your level of heaven.

Intention and Protection

The intention for this journey is to travel to a level of heaven and ask for a healing. For protection, you can say your own phrase or this one: "Please help me to travel safely to and from a level of heaven and receive a healing. Thank you."

Healing Journey

Get ready as you know how and start your recording. Find yourself following the drum to your path in the Middle World and up to the high place. Meet a guide or teacher and journey together through the sun to a level of heaven. Once you land, follow your intuition to the place where you will receive a healing, and ask for a spirit being to come who wants to offer a healing. Be aware of where you are and see who comes.

Take in everything you can: the setting, the one doing the healing, the experience of healing, and let yourself receive this healing fully. When it feels complete, see if you need to say anything, or if they have a message for you.

As the drum speeds up, know that it is time to leave for now, but that you can return any time. Thank your healer and any other spirit beings that are present and say good-bye for now. Make your way back to your helper and fly back through the sun to the Middle

World. Climb down and onto your path, and with a few deep breaths, feel yourself coming back to this world. When ready, open your eyes.

. . . .

Check-In

Who goes with you to the Upper World?

Where do you go within the Upper World to receive your healing?

Who is it that comes to help heal you?

What do you want to heal, and what kind of healing do you receive?

How do you feel during the healing and afterward?

. . . .

Becoming Light

A ray of light comes down and I fly within this beam up higher and higher into space, and suddenly I crash right into a star that blows up into a million pieces and its fragments flow inside me. I grow into a new star with such bright light that it penetrates hearts, the land, the sea, starfish and babies alike. I fall down, down to earth and receive this message: "You are a star being, filled with light, and your task is to bring

light to the world, to help heal the sick, help the blind
see, the maimed walk, to restore faith to those who are
lost. Your healing vibration is increased tenfold, and
you will feel the power in your hands. We are counting
on you!"

In the journey above, I soared into the star nation and filled with light. Right after this experience, I began studying Reiki and the Reconnection and became an energy healer. Around the same time, a body worker told me my hands are very hot and send off so much energy that I should harness this gift and become a healer. And I have.

For the last journey in this chapter, you are invited to become pure light. To do this you can journey to the Upper World and then set the intention to experience the feeling of becoming light. I like the description that energy is densely packed light, that the energy of light is a physical vibration. We know through research in quantum physics that everything is energy; everything is vibrating at a frequency, including us.

Being able to become light has happened to me several times, both in the Upper World and the Middle World, especially when visiting stars, planets, the moon, and all the realms in the Upper World as presented in chapter 5. Such an experience may help you, as it has me, to believe without a doubt that we have spirits or soul essences that are not material. They are pure energy, pure vibration, and pure light.

Intention and Protection

Set the intention for this journey to go to one of the levels of heaven, and while there, intend that you experience becoming light. For protection, you can say, "Please help me go to a level of heaven and experience being light, going and returning safely. Thank you."

Journey of Light

Start the drumming recording and begin to journey when you feel relaxed and ready. You might say your intention and your protection statement as you go into trance. See your path in the Middle World and climb up. Meet a guide, teacher, or other spirit perfect for your journey to become light.

Follow your intuition closely and find yourself journeying into light or becoming light either on your travels to the Upper World or while in your level of heaven. As you become light, notice the energy within you and around you, and feel the frequency of your soul's essence. Just enjoy this sensation. Use all your senses to experience this transfiguration in order to record it later.

When the drum speeds up, it is time to come back to the Middle World, first thanking your allies for this experience with light, and then coming back through the sun to your place of power. Once there, climb down and feel the earth beneath your feet as you walk your path. Breathe in this earth energy, up, all the way up through your body until you feel grounded and solid. Take several deep breaths, and, when ready, open your eyes. If you are feeling a bit spacey, take a few deep breaths, feel your feet on the floor, and drink a glass of water to feel more grounded.

Check-In

Were you able to become the light? If so, describe this experience.

Did you receive any messages, either verbal or non-verbal, on this journey?

How do you feel now that you are back in ordinary reality? Is anything different?

Insight *to* Action

What have you learned in this chapter that you can use to improve your life here? What action are you ready to take to transform your life in amazing ways?

Deeper and Higher

Here at the end of chapter 6 my hope is that you feel expanded, that you feel richer and fuller from your journeys in this part of the book. As I mentioned earlier, the last few chapters are designed to take you deeper, to allow you to experience higher dimensions, to meet loving spirits that only want to help you reach your highest potential. By completing this chapter you are doing just that, realizing more and more who you are in the deepest sense, why you are here, and what it is you are meant to do.

❧ 7 ❧

Loved Ones

You help me understand
there is no death
the soul and love limitless,
timeless, endless,
our spirits joined for eternity.

Now your body may be ash,
but our spirits meet in heaven
where we walk a white sand beach
hand in hand
making tantric love
and spiraling together
in a swirling, pulsing wave of amber light.

We are immortal.

—From my poem "Immortal"

The above poem may surprise you, that it is possible to spend time with a loved one in a level of heaven, and not just spend time, but hold hands, walk along a beach, make love, and spiral together into light! In all honesty, I had no idea this was possible either, until it happened, and not just once. I've met Tom at least weekly for over two years. Each time is slightly different, and we are able to join our energy in every way possible. Actually, this doesn't surprise me when I think about our union on earth; at times when we were physically apart, we would feel each other's energy and even feel as if we were making love. We called it making love in the ether, and now we still do.

Swan carries me to the Upper World and a level of heaven. I see my spirit family in two lines, with hands raised in an arch, fingers touching. I sense I am to walk beneath them and as I do, they smile, sing, embrace me, and make me feel completely loved and welcomed.

At the end of the line, hidden at first, is my husband Tom, laughing and so delighted that he's surprised me. Dressed in his white wedding shirt with little green palm trees, brown hair to his shoulders, he looks just as I remember him when we married. He enfolds me in his arms, lifting me off the ground and swinging me around. With everyone clapping and cheering, we walk down the beach holding hands, running up a sand dune to a crystal temple at the top. In front of the door and through the threshold are scattered red rose petals inviting us in.

We stand in the temple, with golden light pouring through an open ceiling, and there are angels all around. Tom tells me we are renewing our vows and we begin to speak to one another of our immortal love.

Since this journey to a level of heaven, I've visited my loved ones dozens of times, and it is always a heartfelt reunion. In this chapter you will be invited to connect with the energy of those you love and visit them in the spirit world. The first journeys will be to soul mates, lovers, spouses, and partners who have passed on. Then, you will also be able to meet with loved ones such as grandparents, parents, siblings, children, other relatives, friends, colleagues, animal companions, and anyone you were close to and miss.

At times these loved ones may not come when you invite them. This isn't because they don't love you or want to be with you. As souls they have their own work to do, their own process of transformation. Several times my husband has been busy doing the work he needs to do for his own growth, and he can't meet me. Also, after my mother's death, I was unable to connect with her for a few years. She was busy moving through her own progression as a soul. Now, and for the past few years, I do see her and spend time with her, in the level of heaven with my soul family.

You may also meet relatives, ancestors, or descendants that are new to you, as my grandmother was to me. These meetings either in the Middle World or in an Upper World will hopefully help you feel more accepting and at peace, knowing where your loved ones are.

You will know from direct shamanic experience that there is no death and nothing to fear.

At this point you may be asking where your loved ones might be, if they can be met in your place of power, or in the Upper World in a level of heaven. Recently shamanic teacher Hank Wesselman told me that he believes departed souls are mostly in the Middle World. I remember his telling me previously that loved ones can remain in the Middle World for up to one hundred years. Here they are transitioning, working out whatever they need to before moving on. This latest discussion puzzled me because my husband Tom definitely meets me in the Upper World where my soul family and divine teachers appear. At one point I asked Tom how he can travel back and forth between the Middle and Upper Worlds and he told me, "I'm a spirit and not bound by time or space. I can travel freely between the worlds."

According to Sandra Ingerman and Hank Wesselman in *Awakening to the Spirit World*, mystics, visionaries, and shamans from all parts of the world agree that discarnate souls spend time in what has been called the bardo, Purgatory, the dream state, the waiting place, The Middle World, and so on. Tibetans believe that this time in the bardo is about forty days, and relatives can say a long prayer for the deceased from *The Tibetan Book of the Dead* to help a soul transition. After completing a "life-review," the deceased ascends with a higher spirit into the Upper World, where it merges with its higher self and its source.[48]

This Tibetan explanation regarding forty days of transition makes sense in terms of my connection with my husband; he spent the time he needed in the in-between state of the Middle World, and has now moved on more freely to and between other levels. Now for over a year he is in higher realms, and when journeying I meet him in my level of heaven.

In the same text by Ingerman and Wesselman, Alberto Villoldo says, "In the Amazon there are shamans who claim to have journeyed beyond death. Their stories are very similar to ones told by Tibetans who have mapped the journey across thousands of years." Villoldo goes on to describe this place beyond death as the dawn of a new world where a person is surrounded by light and becomes the light.[49]

I have personally experienced what Villoldo describes, and my journey as a light being is described in chapter 6. I agree with the Inca that we carry the luminous within us to a universal light and merge in oneness. Now you have the opportunity to visit your own loved ones in a luminous world of spirit.

• •

Check-In

What thoughts and feelings are arising about your own departed loved ones?

Have you ever had dreams, visions, or visitations from those who have passed on?

Where do you think departed souls go?

• •

Mates in Spirit

If your soul mate, life partner, spouse, or lover has died, my heart goes out to you. I know how it feels when the person you love most is no longer here physically. What I've discovered since my husband's death is that we are forever connected to our loved ones, as expressed in the above poem and journey. By being conscious both in daily life and when doing journeywork, we can feel their presence, connect with their energy, and spend time with them in the middle and upper realms.

What I've also found is that the closer you have been to this individual, the more opportunity there is for connection. You have already merged your energy during time together, and this energy continues after death. Yes, the body dies and is either buried or cremated, but the spirit or soul of this person lives on and is infinite, not finite. The person you love and feel you've lost is not truly gone; who they are has just changed form, from a physical body to the energy of love, light, and all the qualities within them.

Think for a moment about a loved one who has passed on, and recall feeling energy pass between you. Some people call this energy connection, chemistry, or a "vibe," but whatever you call it, it is like a wavelength or a vibration between you. Perhaps you've felt this energy when first meeting someone, while shaking hands or looking into someone's eyes; or you may have felt this vibration with your mate or lover, especially while holding hands, embracing, kissing, or making love.

From personal experience and from talking with clients and colleagues, as well as speaking with physicists, I know that energy connection is real and continues after death. What you felt with the person you love does not die with them; it continues, and you can still feel their essence, sometimes more strongly now that they no longer have a body. They can be free to be pure energy and often seem lighter, more joyful, and at peace.

To illustrate, my husband Tom was a very playful, spontaneous, creative, and inspiring man. Unfortunately, by the end of his life, after six years of illness, he no longer could be this person due to intense pain and immobility. Now when I see him in a level of heaven, his true nature is totally free to express itself. He is smiling, laughing, wanting to run with me and tumble down sand dunes. Recently, we danced barefoot on the sand and he twirled and spun me as he once did on every dance floor! Now, without a body, my husband and your loved ones can return to their original essence and truly shine.

. . . .

Check-In

Who is your soul mate, partner, lover, or the departed loved one you miss most? Write their name in your journal.

Now, close your eyes, sit comfortably, take a deep breath, and let yourself relax. With eyes closed, let images of your loved one come, especially ones when the two of you were together and very happy. Envision him or her in as much detail as possible. It's okay to cry and feel whatever is coming up.

Really connect with the energy of that time and place, and especially with your mate or loved one. When you feel complete, take a breath or two and open your eyes.

Write down what came to you in your visualization.

● ●

Connection in Real Time

Before journeying to spirit worlds to meet departed loved ones, it helps to connect with their energy right here in the ordinary world.

From my window I see avocados dangling from the tree over an outbuilding. I love avocados and want to climb on the roof and pick some. I set the ladder against the wall and before I can climb, feel my husband's presence and hear his voice, "I don't want you on this ladder; you could fall and end up in a wheelchair." I still want to climb, so I ask him to protect me, to steady the ladder and help me remain safe. I set my feet on each metal rung and I feel strong and powerful as I step onto asphalt tiles. The avocados are waiting and I fill my shirt with at least a dozen. I again can feel my husband's strong hands holding the ladder as I climb down. I thank him as I walk into the house with my green treasures.

On another occasion I felt Tom with me very strongly and even felt his touch. I decided to design the cover for a new book, *Our Spirits Dance: Poetry of Soul Mates*, love poems my husband and I wrote. I hadn't painted for at least six years, but dusting off brushes and spraying water on my dried paints, I felt no hesitation and my hand seemed guided by Tom's spirit. Within minutes the painting was done. I have no doubt that the two of us painted it, using images from the title poem that became the book's cover art.

Practice

If you meditate or close your eyes to relax during the day, just consciously intend to feel a departed loved one's presence. In addition, it may help to hold something of theirs such as clothing or a favorite object, or it may help to look at a photo or listen to a special song.

Sit or lie down somewhere comfortable and close your eyes. While holding a special object or just by thinking of your loved one, let yourself invite in their energy. Sense your loved one's energy and feel them close.

Write about your experience in your journal.

Special Places

Also, any time you visit a favorite place, a restaurant, park, store, and so on, notice if you feel your loved one's presence. This happens to me when walking in our garden, in a hardware store, or in the restaurant where we always had breakfast. Pay close attention to a feeling or energy in a familiar place or in your body when visiting somewhere special to the two of you.

Check-In

Write about your visit to a well-loved place and record anything you felt.

Messages from Loved Ones

I am outside in our courtyard, trimming branches from the peach tree. As I look up at clusters of pink flowers, I find myself saying aloud, "I wish you were here to see all these incredible blossoms; this is going to be quite a year for fruit!" Within seconds I hear Tom's voice, "I am here! Hey, are you going to make jam this year?"

His presence and voice took me by surprise this time; I'd momentarily forgotten he is right here all the time and I can hear messages from him when I pay attention. So besides feeling your spirit mate or loved one's energy, you can be more receptive to receiving messages directly from him or her. In addition, you might get signs from your loved one through nature, from butterflies and hawks to coyotes and foxes crossing the road. Look up the meanings of these beings and see if their presence is sending a message from someone you love.

Besides having nature as a messenger, people can call just at the right time, or we receive a letter or email from someone saying the most comforting and helpful words, that sound a lot like what our partners might say.

At times, a song might come on the radio or play in a store or elevator that is one the two of you loved. This has happened so many times to me that I am now sure that Tom "sent" these messages.

Practice by thinking thoughts and questions or speaking them aloud, and see if you hear an answer or comment from your loved one. When I'm alone at home I sometimes speak out loud to Tom and I hear him answer in my head. Keep noticing any messages from loved ones that come directly or from the world around you.

• •

Check-In

Write down any messages from music, nature, other people, or direct comments that you "hear" your departed loved one say.

• •

Written Dialogue

In a final exercise, use your journal to create a written dialogue between you and your dear one. All you do is begin a conversation in writing by asking a question or saying how you feel or what you need. You can hear their words in your head and then write them down. This is how I began a written dialogue, and as Tom "spoke," I just wrote down the words that came automatically without thinking. They just poured out. It helps not to think, just letting the pen flow and not lifting it from the page. Keep writing until it feels finished and then ask another question or say what it is you are feeling and need.

You might start with "How are you?" Write what you hear them say.

What's it like where you are?

I've been feeling . . .

I've wanted to ask you . . .

You can feel your loved one as much as you want to. Remember, loving spirits are ready to be with us and support us; all we need to do is ask. The more you speak with your spirit mate or loved one in your mind, the more he or she will answer you. As you become more open to these dialogues and connections, the more they will happen. And, no, you're not crazy; you are demonstrating that you are more than your physical body; you are an energy, spirit, and soul, able to commune with another energetic spirit.

Meeting a Partner or Other Loved One

This first journey is to a mate or lover who has passed on. Often when we have been partnered with someone and have been close, it is easier to feel their energy and to meet with him or her in middle or upper levels. If this exercise does not apply to you, feel free to go ahead to the next section or to journey here to anyone you love who has passed into spirit.

Intention and Protection

Say your intention silently or aloud: "I want to journey to the Middle and Upper Worlds and visit with (person's name)."

Next, if your intuition indicates that you are meeting your loved one in your Middle World, then you will journey there and invite them in. Otherwise, once you reach your place of power you need to climb up to your high place and then a spirit helper or object will appear to take you to the Upper World.

Before you journey, you can say a phrase of protection or hold a stone or sacred object for grounding.

Journey

Listen to the drum and journey to your special place in the Middle World. Once you arrive, follow your intuition about whether your mate is here in the Middle World or is now in the Upper World. If you sense your loved one is still here, then invite him or her to join you. Follow further instructions about how to connect with them in the paragraphs that follow. If you sense that your partner is in a level of heaven, then travel through the sun to your level of heaven.

You may see your soul family or teachers, and others you have met previously. As you walk in this Upper World, intend that your mate or loved one appear. There is no guarantee that he or she will be here this time, but my guess is that they will come, or another being will appear who wants to connect with you.

This journey is especially for those of you who wish to connect with your departed mates. Once you see them approaching, either in the middle or upper worlds, connect in whatever way seems right for the two of you. Spend time together until the drum speeds up and it is time to return. Say your good-byes, and thank your loved one for coming, knowing you can return any time now, and begin to walk back to the place where your "transportation" waits. Come back the same way through the sun, and then return to the path in the Middle World, breathe yourself back, and, when ready, open your eyes.

* *

Check-In

Did you meet a loved one in the Middle or Upper World?

Who came when you invited in your partner or someone you love?

Describe your experience together.

* *

Other Relatives in Spirit

As the sun rises, it wraps me in a warm cocoon, and we fly swiftly to my level of heaven, landing on the beach. All I know is that I need my mother. I go to her and she puts her arms around me. We find a beautiful

glider on a porch where I lie with my head in her lap
and she strokes my hair. She softly sings to me and
soothes me with her hands and her voice. She tells me
that I'm never alone, that those who love me are with
me all the time.

You, too, can visit another departed relative, whether a parent, grandparent, brother, sister, child, or other relative, and feel connected and supported as I did with my mother. This journey is to visit a relative other than your mate or partner. Think about all those you love who have passed on. Perhaps your beloved spirit beings are also aunts, uncles, cousins, and any others you consider family. If you are adopted, you can ask to visit with either family, as one of my clients did recently.

Check-In

Who do you miss of your family members that have transitioned?

How were they important in your life?

Is there anything you want to tell them or ask them during your reunion?

Practice

When you have the time, close your eyes and take a breath in, letting yourself relax. Allow yourself to daydream about relatives you love who have passed on. Let faces come, and perhaps memories of times together. If you feel like crying, go ahead and do so. Recall a time together when this person was healthy and doing well. Use all your senses and take in everything about them, from their appearance to your conversations and what you enjoy doing together.

Once your time together feels complete, bring back these memories and write about them in your journal.

The Relatives That Appear

If a beloved relative has recently died, this is the perfect opportunity and person to start with. When souls are newly spirits, many times they are closer to us and we can connect with them more easily.

You may have already seen some of your relatives in the previous chapters when journeying to your place of power and then later to a level of heaven. Spirit beings can move easily between the worlds. I have seen my parents, husband, Jesus, ancestors, guides, and teachers in both the Middle and Upper Worlds. So don't be surprised if you see someone in more than one world.

Intention and Protection

Your intention for this journey is to travel to your place of power and then perhaps to a level of heaven, to meet one or more relatives. "I wish to meet (name of person), but am open to any relative who loves me." For protection, you may ask to be guided to the Upper World safely and to be brought back with ease.

Journey to Meet a Relative

This journey is not to a mate or lover, but don't be surprised if your partner also shows up (if they did in the previous journey). Recently, I went to spend time with my parents and Tom was waiting to see me. Once you make contact with beings in the spirit world, they often are there waiting for you. They love you and are happy when you visit.

Let the drum take you into trance and imagine yourself in your personal place of power. Follow your intuition as to whether to invite in a loved one here in the Middle World or in the Upper World. If you decide to invite your departed relative into your place of power, do so now. Spend time together and receive as much wisdom as you can.

If your intuition says to journey upward, meet your "transportation," pass through the sun's energy, and then arrive in your level of heaven. Begin walking in the Upper World, expecting someone to come toward you. Again, the relative you wish to visit may be here, but someone else could arrive instead. Spend time with this person, and do whatever feels right to you both.

You might want to ask how the relative is doing, even what jobs or tasks are assigned in heaven. You can ask questions you never asked when they were alive. Often it is helpful to ask for feedback about your life and what they think could help you.

When the drum speeds up, say good-bye to your loved one(s) and make your way back to the helper waiting for you. Come back the same way you went, and find yourself descending and landing somewhere in your place of power. If you chose to remain in your Middle World, now walk out of your sacred place and onto your path. Take a breath in and breathe yourself back to ordinary reality. When you are ready, open your eyes.

. . . .

Check-In

Did you choose to meet with your departed relative in the Middle or Upper Worlds?

Did someone come to meet you? If so, who appeared? Describe your time together.

What insights did you receive from this encounter?

. . . .

Friends

When I ask loving departed friends to come through my waterfall, Shelley appears (she transitioned twenty years ago). Shelley always looked radiant in life, and now she is nearly pure light. She takes my hand and says we are going to the Upper World. We fly through the sun holding hands, then land in an alpine meadow of green grass and flowers. Ahead is a white-capped mountain.

We climb to the top of the mountain, and in front of us is a dawn sky, full of pale gold light and rosy clouds. I am awestruck by this beauty. Shelley nods as if reading my mind and says, "Yes, this is heaven, and you can see why I don't miss being in my body. Remember how much pain I was in, and you were there when the ambulance came to take me to the nursing home." I do recall how sad Shelley looked as they carried her out on a gurney; she was looking back at her home, knowing she was never coming back. I see how happy Shelley is now, how free and full of light and peace.

Seeing Shelley in the spirit worlds confirms for me once again that our departed loved ones are exactly where they need to be and are doing fine. After this journey, I, too, felt more at peace, seeing that I can enjoy my life now without fear, knowing that all is well here and in the world to come.

Perhaps there are friends you miss who have passed on to the world of spirit. Just think for a moment about the friends you love and miss.

List your departed friends in your journal. Who is it you especially want to see and why?

Intention and Protection

The intention for this journey is to first go to your Middle World and invite in any departed friends who love you, knowing that you may stay in your sacred place or go to the Upper World. For protection just say whatever you wish.

Journey to Meet a Friend

Prepare as you usually do, letting the drum lead you to your path and place of power in the Middle World. Once there, follow your intuition to the place where you expect to meet departed friends, either here in your place of power or perhaps in an Upper World. If you are going to the Upper World, find your way up, wait for a helper to arrive, and then travel through the sun to the higher realms. Once settled in the world of your choice, invite in a friend who loves you and wants to connect.

After setting this intention, just see who shows up, letting the experience unfold naturally. Once a friend arrives, connect and talk about whatever is important to both of you. Enjoy your time together.

When the drumming speeds up, thank your friend and say good-bye. Come all the way back to your starting place on the path, take a few deep breaths, stretch, and, when ready, open your eyes.

··

Check-In

Did you stay in your Middle World to invite in a friend, or did you go to an Upper World?

Who showed up when you called, and how does this friend appear now?

What did the two of you talk about?

How do you feel now that you have visited with your friend?

··

Animal Companions

I arrive in my level of heaven and walk barefoot on the sand, as green waves tumble in the surf. In the distance I see something running toward me at great speed, like a red dervish. As it gets closer, I see it is our family dog, Rusty, his floppy, Irish Setter ears bouncing up and down, tongue hanging out, and root-beer-colored eyes shining. He gets to me, and just as in life, he knocks me down, all eighty-five pounds landing on my chest. He's knocked the wind out of me, but soon has me laughing as he washes my face with a sandpaper tongue. I throw my arms around him and we wrestle in the sand. I love this dog, and love seeing him so healthy. He is in his prime once again here in heaven.

It may not be just people you miss, but your dogs, cats, and other sweet beings that have been your animal companions. I know that at times in my life my animals have been my favorite friends, so loving and devoted, so present, uncomplaining, and patient. I have especially missed my cats Finny and Mitzy, and my childhood dog Rusty.

I've missed him so much. How amazing is it that I can now visit Rusty any time? He is vibrant and whole, youthful and as full of mischief as he was here.

Check-In

Do you have animal companions you would like to visit in a level of heaven? Write their names in your journal.

What do you miss about your animal friends?

What do you hope happens if you are able to connect again?

Practice

Close your eyes for a moment and recall a happy time with a special animal companion. Remember how this beloved pet looked, where you were, and what you were doing. Just breathe in the love and connection. When the experience feels complete, take a breath in and come back to the room, open your eyes, and write down your memories.

Intention and Protection

In this journey your intention is to invite in a departed animal companion. Again, follow your intuition, and of course, you can do two journeys or as many as you like to animals you love and miss, or invite them all at once! Your intention is to first go to your Middle World and then decide whether to meet your loved one there or in the Upper World. For protection, just say whatever works for you.

Animal Companion Journey

Listen to the drum and envision yourself on your path and then in your place of power. Think about the animal companion you wish to invite and follow intuition about whether to do this here or in a level of heaven. In either place, ask this special animal friend to join you and then see what happens next. If your pet arrives or a different one comes, go ahead and have fun and perhaps a dialogue. Remember that anything they say will come to you in your mind. When the drumming speeds up, say your thanks and good-byes and make your way back to your path, and with a few deep breaths, open your eyes.

Check-In

Did an animal companion show up? Describe this being and your encounter.

Did you have any realizations during or after this journey?

Insight *to* Action

What have you discovered during this chapter that you could use in your life here? What action can you take to bring your insights to fruition?

Conclusions

We've come to the end of chapter 7, and I hope you feel comforted and more at peace after visiting those you love. Knowing where our partners, relatives, and other loved ones have gone, and discovering they are fine, can bring such a deep sense of relief. You also may have begun to heal your own issues about death and can now live life more consciously, knowing that the grave is not the end, and that your spirit and the spirits of loved ones are immortal.

Now you have the opportunity to apply all you've learned in the book to your life in chapter 8, "Bringing Heaven Home." This is the gift of visiting spirit realms, including a level of heaven, while still alive. You have a chance to change what is no longer working, either within you or in your life. You have a chance to become more fulfilled, and to live your soul's purpose in this life-time. All the interactions with your helpers, spirit allies, teachers, guides, and now your loved ones can assist you to take action and create your own heaven on earth.

❧ 8 ❧

Bringing Heaven Home

What is it that makes you happy?
What is it that sets you free?
Is it money and the things it can buy you,
or is love and connection the key?

Do you know? Can you feel
The truth? What is real?

Just listen to the voice inside you.
Just listen to your soul.
Then follow whatever it tells you.
And you will feel more whole.
And you will feel more whole.

—From my song "What Is Real?"

I fly on my horse White Magic up to the moon and across the Bridge of Luminosity to Arianrhod's palace. Inside one of the rooms jewels glisten on each wall. The Goddess gives me an aquamarine and tells me to swallow it to give me inner illumination. All I need to do is visualize the glowing jewel inside me, radiating the truth, and my inner light of intuition will guide my way. She suggests I stay balanced and strong, knowing what it is I need and then taking action. She takes me to the Weaver, Spider Woman, who says I can write a book about shamanism with my own journeys in each chapter, and teach people how to find the truth inside them: "Weave the magic of the dream for readers to fall into."

How would you like to create a heavenly life? You can do this, as the song suggests, by discovering what makes you happy and free, healing your life issues, listening to the inner voice of your soul, becoming healthy and whole, and knowing and feeling the truth of what is real in your life. Welcome to our last chapter, "Bringing Heaven Home." Here you will take all you've realized in the previous pages and apply it to your current life. Isn't this the ultimate gift of going to heaven before you die—using the insights from loving spirits and your own higher self to transform your life right now?

The date of the above journal entry was 2005. As always, my guides and teachers encourage and suggest a possible course of action, and I listen, even if it is a decade later! Here I am writing this book about shamanism with my own journeys in each chapter as they predicted. I appreciate my spirit beings for their insight, and I might add, patience, waiting for me to become ready, and then continuing to help me fulfill my purpose.

You, too, are being encouraged by your own spirit allies, animal helpers, ancestors, guides, and teachers to listen to shared wisdom and take action that can and will change your life in miraculous ways. This chapter is about gathering all the messages from earlier journeys and creating plans to bring them to fruition in your ordinary life.

Overview of Your Life

In this journey you can assess your current life with the help of your spirit beings. This exercise can provide clarity about what is going well and not as well in your ordinary life. In this assessment journey, notice how happy you are with your spiritual practice, physical and emotional health, relationships, professional work or service, creativity, and leisure time.

Intention and Protection

The intention for this journey is to go to your sacred place in the Middle World and invite in a spirit ally, ancestor, guide, or teacher to help you find clarity about your life. When you arrive, follow your intuition about whether to stay here or journey to the Lower or Upper World for this overview. You might say something like, "Please help me discover what areas of my life are working well and which ones may need to change." For protection, just say whatever feels right to you.

Journey for Clarity

Settle in and when you feel relaxed and ready, use the drum to take you to the path to your place of power.

Now, following your intuition, decide if you are going to stay here or journey up or down to meet with spirit beings. If you stay in the Middle World, invite in the perfect loving being to help you assess your real life. This may be a familiar spirit ally or perhaps a new one. If you travel up or down, then invite in a loving being to help you there.

When this helper arrives, ask for clarity about your current life, or ask more specific questions about parts of your life, as listed earlier. Remember that spirit beings are not going to tell you what to do. They are going to suggest, encourage, and offer, but will not take away your own intuitive power to choose.

You may even bring up ways you feel happy and ways you don't, or ask how you can feel more fulfilled and how you can live your purpose. You could also discuss what seems to be working in your life in certain areas and what doesn't feel in sync. Be as specific as you wish, and receive the perfect guidance.

When the drumming speeds up, say good-bye and thank you and make your way to your path and back to the place you began. Take a few deep breaths, move your hands and feet, and, when ready, open your eyes.

Check-In

Where did you end up in this journey?

Who showed up when you asked for someone to appear?

What did you ask this spirit being, and what did they offer?

Overall, what is working well in your life that you want to keep?

What is not working as well that you want to change?

A Life Plan of Action

Now you're ready to write an action plan for your life using all the discoveries you've made in previous journeys. You can revisit your check-ins from other chapters and use your answers to help with this process. Also, look at the "Insight to Action" section at the end of each chapter for a summary of your realizations. Writing a life plan means stating what you are actually going to do in order to improve and enhance each part of your life. You could write down the general ideas about what you wish to keep or change or set specific goals with the dates to begin.

To take action, we first set a goal, but then must follow through with the steps to achieve it. It helps to follow intuition, do what makes us happy, tell the truth to ourselves and others, set boundaries, and generally be ready and willing to act by making that phone call, doing the research, writing the email, talking to people, showing up where we need to, beginning a new habit or a practice, then following through with what we've begun.

Some of us don't like change and resist it even though our old life isn't working and we aren't happy. This is mostly done out of fear: fear of losing something such as security, making the wrong choice, or being worse off after we make the change. The key is to trust in our higher self that is speaking to us through intuition, and when we do, things line up with the universe. Taking that first step in making a change is often the hardest, but our ultimate happiness is the reward.

What is it you want to be, do, or have, and what are you going to do from this moment forward to attain it? You might write what you are doing now if it's working well, or add or change some things. What is it I want in the following areas?

Spiritual Practice

Physical and Emotional Health

Relationships

Professional Work or Service

Creativity

Leisure Time

Please write your goals for each area in your journal.

Daily Formula for Happiness

Another tool to help restructure your life for the most joy is the "Daily Formula for Happiness." You can use the general categories in the above section to help you find your formula. Here's my formula to give you an idea of how I ideally spend my days. This doesn't mean that every day is exactly like this, but I strive to have most of these elements so I feel good about myself and my life:

> *Prayer and meditation + solitude + time outdoors + physical activity + quality time or communication with at least one friend or family member + nutritious food + doing my job well + doing something creative like painting, songwriting, or writing a poem + reading or entertainment + restful sleep.*

You might notice that several of these can be done together. I can go to the ocean and meditate, be in solitude, be outside, walk on the beach, and even write in my journal or eat a healthy lunch, all in the same outing. You could also spend time with loved ones having a great meal, watching a good movie together, and communicating about what is important to you. As you create your own formula, notice where you can combine different parts for the greatest joy and efficiency. You can tell that you have the right formula by how you feel at the end of each day. Ideally, you feel fulfilled and grateful for your awesome life. Listen to your higher self through intuition and write your formula in your journal.

The idea is to strive for what feels best, but not to feel guilty if you don't achieve it every day. Just know that you feel better when you have some time for you, or you really feel healthy when you eat well or go to yoga, and some days it doesn't happen. And you can put your formula into play the following day. It's just about assessing and correcting, not judging and punishing. It's about whatever works for you and your happiness.

The End Is Not the End

As this chapter ends and the book comes to a close, I have faith that you will keep journeying and evolving for many years to come. My hope is that you are happy and living with passionate purpose; that you change whatever is no longer serving you and create an amazing life full of joy and fulfillment.

It has been such an honor to walk with you on this path. It has been my deepest desire to help you overcome any fear of death, to truly know that there is no death, that you and your loved ones are immortal, and that "you don't have to die to go to heaven." You can find heaven in your spirit worlds and with all the beings that love you, and you are also creating your own heaven right here. I wish you many blessings on the journey that is your life.

Acknowledgments

A book is written by more than one person. A community of people and a lifetime of experiences contribute to its birthing. First, I want to thank my teachers in transcendental meditation for helping me develop a practice that has spanned nearly forty years. For me, meditation has been the gate into the garden of shamanic journeywork.

I'd like to thank author Alexandra Kennedy for introducing me to shamanic journeying, and Michael Harner for his experiential shamanic trainings. Through the teachings of Incan shamanism, Alberto Villoldo helped me further understand my own path as a shamanic practitioner. I learned the practices of Hawaiian shamanism from Hank Wesselman and Jill Kuykendall, and have used these teachings for my own transformation and to help my clients. I am so grateful for all these teachers.

I especially want to thank Jan Johnson, publisher at Red Wheel/Weiser, for her enthusiastic support of this project, and for offering wise counsel along the way. Also, I'd like to acknowledge the staff at Red Wheel/Weiser for being so proactive and professional—especially Kim Ehart, Rachel Leach, Eryn Carter, and Bonni Hamilton. You are a great team.

To the listeners of my radio show "We Carry the Light," *www.transformationtalkradio.com*, thanks for being excited about the show and my new book, and thanks to Dr. Pat, brilliant host and network head, for her mentoring and enthusiastic support.

Endnotes

Introduction

1. Sandra Ingerman and Hank Wesselman, *Awakening to the Spirit World: The Shamanic Path of Direct Revelation* (Boulder, CO: Sounds True, Inc., 2010), 30.

Chapter 1

2. See various sources regarding the life of Lao Tzu, such as *www.thetao.info*.

3. See various sources about the Celtic moon goddess Arianrhod, such as *www.feminismandreligion.com*.

4. See a variety of books and sites about the Hindu hero and god Lord Rama, such as the texts *Arrow of the Blue-Skinned God: Retracing the Ramayana through India* by Jonah Blank; *Sri Rama as God Almighty: Adhyatma Ramayanam* by S. Balakrishnan; *The Rámáyan of Válmíkí* by Válmíkí; and sites such as *www.hindunet.org*.

5. See origins of the name Menana on sites about Hindi names and in the history of South Africa's settlement of people from India in Tongan communities.

Chapter 3

6. See numerous sites about the god Ganesh, especially the book by James H. Bae, *Ganesh: Removing the Obstacles* (San Rafael, CA: Om Books, 2008).

7. Rachel Pollack, *The Kabbalah Tree: A Journey of Balance & Growth* (Woodbury, MN: Llewellyn Publications, 2010).

8. Cherry Gilchrist, *Russian Magic: Living Folk Traditions of an Enchanted Landscape* (Wheaton, IL: Quest Books, 2009).

9. Pollack, *The Kabbalah Tree*, 3–5, 134.

10. Genesis 2:9 and 3:24.

11. Proverbs 3:18, 11:30, 13:12, and 15:4.

12. Enoch 25:4–6.

13. Revelation 2:7, 22:2.

14. See books and sites about the Tree of life in world cultures, such as *The Tree of Life: From Eden to Eternity*, edited by John W. Welch and Donald W. Parry, and the site *artof4elements.com/entry/43/tree-of-life*, as well as the film by director Terrence Malick, *The Tree of Life*, about grace, beauty, suffering, good and evil, and more.

15. Genesis 28:13 and Pollack, *The Kabbalah Tree*, 4–5.

16. Ted Andrews, *Animal Speak: The Spiritual & Magical Powers of Creatures Great & Small* (St. Paul, MN: Llewellyn Publications, 1996), 141.

17. Andrews, *Animal Speak*, 152.

18. Andrews, *Animal Speak*, 196.

19. See various sites about the story of Pegasus and Bellerophon, such as *www.greekmythology.com*. One of my favorite writers about Greek mythology is Edith Hamilton. Her best books are *Mythology: Timeless Tales of Gods and Heroes* and *The Greek Way*.

20. Search for more information regarding the winged serpent at *www.atlantisquest.com/Quetzal.html* and *http://www.bibliotecapleyades.net/serpents_dragons/boulay-index-en.htm*.

Chapter 4

21. See books and sites about the constellations, such as Giuseppe Maria Sesti's book *The Glorious Constellations: History and Mythology*, or *The Book of Constellations: Discover the Secrets in the Stars* by Robin Kerrod, or *A Walk through the Heavens: A Guide to Stars and Constellations and Their Legends* by Milton D. Heifetz and Wil Tirion. Sites include *www.atlantisquest.com/Quetzal.html*.

22. Learn more about the constellation Virgo at *www.topastronomer.com* or *www.oneminuteastronomer.com*.

23. Algonquian cultural views and names for the moon can be found at *www.windows2universe.org*.

24. Background about Soma, the Hindu moon god, can be found at *www.pantheon.org/articles/s/soma.html*.

25. Arianrhod, the Celtic moon goddess, can be further researched at *www.feminismandreligion.com* and *www.thewhitegoddess.co.uk*.

26. See Jean Shinoda Bolen's *Artemis: The Indomitable Spirit in Everywoman* to further understand the Greek goddess Artemis. See also the *Thematic Guide to World Mythology* by Lorena Laura Stookey for a comprehensive view of the

Greek moon goddesses Selene and Artemis. Sites include *www.elfinspell.com*, quoting Alexander Murray's *Manual of Mythology*.

27. Go to *http://solarsystem.nasa.gov* to learn more about the sun and solar flares.

28. For more information about the Egyptian sun god Ra, go to *www.crystalinks.com*.

29. To read more about the sun gods riding in chariots in Greek culture, visit *http://www.greeka.com/greece-myths/*.

Chapter 5

30. Read about Shangri-La and see the PBS video at *pbs.org*. To learn more about James Hilton's novel *Lost Horizon* and the origin of Shangri-La, go to *www.sfsite.com/~silverag /hilton.html*.

31. If intrigued by the legends of Lemuria and Atlantis, read Shirley Andrews' *Lemuria and Atlantis: Studying the Past to Survive the Future*.

32. To research more about El Dorado go to *www.rupununi .org/el-dorado*.

33. More about the Greek underworld, Greek views of the afterlife, and Cicero's perspective can be found at *scholarspace.jccc.edu* in a paper by Amy Goodpasture entitled "Depictions (Visions) of the Afterlife."

34. See more about the ancient Egyptian view of the afterlife at *www.egyptpast.com/gods/afterlife.html*.

35. More information about the Hindu and Buddhist perception of the afterlife can be found at *www.sptimmortalityproject .com*.

36. Further information about Buddha's effect on the Hindu belief in reincarnation can be found at *spice.fsi.stanford.edu /docs/introduction_to_buddhism*.

37. To find out more about Jewish views of death and the afterlife go to *www.ourki.org*.

38. Information about the Mormon view of the afterlife can be found at *www.lightplanet.com/mormons/basic/afterlife*.

39. To compare and contrast worldviews of the afterlife and to specifically look at these views from a Catholic and Universalist perspective go to *https://en.wikipedia.org/wiki/ Afterlife*.

40. See the text *Gleanings from the Writings of Bahá'u'lláh* at *http://reference.bahai.org/en/t/b/GWB/* to understand the view of the afterlife in the Bahá'í faith.

Chapter 6

41. For an in-depth presentation of Plato's view of the soul and immortality, read Plato's *Republic* and *Phaedo*. For a brief analysis, go to *www.scandalon.co.uk*.

42. See W. T. S. Thackara's essay "Socrates: Midwife to Our Souls" at *www.theosophy-nw.org*.

43. Ralph Waldo Emerson, *Self-Reliance, the Over-Soul, and Other Essays* (Claremont, CA: Coyote Canyon Press, 2010), 55–57.

44. Deepak Chopra, *Creating Affluence* (San Rafael, CA: Amber Allen, 1998), 90–91.

45. More about Allen Roland and his tenets regarding the Unified Field can be found at *www.allenroland.com*.

46. Visit 9waysmysteryschool.tripod.com to learn more about Pythagoras.

47. More about the Mystery School at Eleusis near Athens, Greece, can be found in Dr. Mara Lynn Keller's work *The Ritual Path of Initiation into the Eleusinian Mysteries* (2009) at *www.ciis.edu/Documents/07_keller.pdf*.

Chapter 7

48. *Awakening to the Spirit World*, 184.

49. *Awakening to the Spirit World*, 185.

About the Author

Dr. Susan Allison is a non-fiction writer and poet and the author of five books: *Conscious Divorce, Breathing Room, Empowered Healer, Our Spirits Dance,* and *You Don't Have to Die to Go to Heaven.* She has advanced degrees in English, history, and psychology, has been trained in hypnotherapy and energy medicine, and is an ordained minister and a songwriter with two CDs: "We Carry the Light" and "Broken Open." Currently, she is a transpersonal psychologist in private practice and uses shamanic journeying, hypnosis, process therapy, and energy medicine to help her clients heal and transform. Dr. Allison also hosts the radio show "We Carry the Light," which airs in Seattle and New York and can be accessed online at *www.transformationtalkradio. com.* When she is not writing, seeing clients, or leading groups, she enjoys a creative life in Santa Cruz, California. She can be contacted at *www.drsusanallison.com.*

To Our Readers

Weiser Books, an imprint of Red Wheel/Weiser, publishes books across the entire spectrum of occult, esoteric, speculative, and New Age subjects. Our mission is to publish quality books that will make a difference in people's lives without advocating any one particular path or field of study. We value the integrity, originality, and depth of knowledge of our authors.

Our readers are our most important resource, and we appreciate your input, suggestions, and ideas about what you would like to see published.

Visit our website at *www.redwheelweiser.com* to learn about our upcoming books and free downloads, and be sure to go to *www.redwheelweiser.com/newsletter* to sign up for newsletters and exclusive offers.

You can also contact us at *info@rwwbooks.com* or at

Red Wheel/Weiser, LLC
65 Parker Street, Suite 7
Newburyport, MA 01950